BEFORE ABRAHAM WAS

I AM

JOHN 8:58

EDWARD D. ANDREWS

BEFORE ABRAHAM WAS
I AM

Two Views on Translating John 8:58

Edward D. Andrews

Christian Publishing House

Cambridge, Ohio

BEFORE ABRAHAM WAS I AM: Two Views on Translating John 8:58

Authored by Edward D Andrews

ISBN-13: **9798617601819**

TRANSLATIONS Referred to in this Publication

Unless otherwise indicated, Scripture quotations are from the *Updated American Standard Version of the Holy Scriptures*, 2020 (UASV). Abbreviations used to designate other translations of the Bible are provided below:

ASV: American Standard Version (1901)

AMP: Amplified Bible (1987)

AT: The Bible – An American Translation (1935)

CEB: Common English Bible (2011)

CEV: Contemporary English Version (1995)

DARBY: Darby Translation (1890)

ERV: Easy to Read Version (2012)

GW: GOD'S WORD Translation (1995)

GNT: Good News Translation (1992)

HCSB: Holman Christian Standard Bible (2003)

JB: The Jerusalem Bible (1966)

JP: The Holy Scriptures According to the Masoretic Text (1917)

KJV: King James Version (1611, 1942)

LEB: Lexham English Bible (LEB)

LXX: Greek Septuagint Version of Hebrew Old Testament (280-150 B.C.E.)

NCV: New Century Version (2005)

NEB: New English Bible (1970)

NLV: New Life Version (1969)

NLT: New Living Translation (2013)

NTB: A New Translation of the Bible (1934)

NASB: New American Standard Bible (1995)

NET: New English Translation (2006) Biblical Studies Press

NIV: New International Version (2011)

NIVI: New International Version Inclusive Language Edition (1996)

NKJV: New King James Version (1982)

NLT: New Living Translation (2007)

NLV: New Language Version (1969)

NRSV: New Revised Standard Version (1989)

PHILIPS: New Testament in Modern English (1958)

REB: Revised English Bible (1989)

RSV: Revised Standard Version (1971)

SEB: Simple English Bible (1980)

TEB: The Emphasised Bible (1897)

TEV: Today's English Version (1976)

TLB: The Living Bible (1971)

TNIV: Today's New International Version (2005)

UASV: Updated American Standard Version (2013-21 Work in progress)[1]

WHNU: Westcott-Hort Greek New Testament / Nestle-Aland Greek New Testament, United Bible Society Greek New Testament (1881, 2012, 1993)

YLT: Young's Literal Translation (1887)

---

[1] The UASV is projected to be completed by 2021. However, we are using verses herein of the books that are completed at present.

PREFACE

The Objective of This Publication

JOHN 8:58 has been one of the most hotly debated verses in the Bible for centuries. For the first time, an impartial, unbiased, objective investigation begins and ends here. *BEFORE ABRAHAM WAS I AM* is for all individuals interested in how **John 8:58** should be translated, as well as how it should be interpreted. The book impartially (objectively) offers the two different translation views on this verse, as well as two different interpretational views. The reader is given the opportunity to see both perspectives, and then, he or she can decide for themselves. The reader does not have to know Biblical Greek, as we have taken every measure to make this small book easy to understand. We have used the Greek interlinear with the English above the Greek. We have translated all the Greek herein. We have tried to define and explain every uncommon term.

Views on translating John 8:58 include NT commentator with the historical setting Kenneth O Gangel, Bible background Clinton E. Arnold and Craig S.

Keener, Exegetical commentator D. A. Carson, NT Greek scholar Daniel B. Wallace, Textual scholar B. F. Westcott, Senior Bible Translator of the NASB Don Wilkins, and Chief Translator of the UASV and textual scholar Edward D. Andrews.

INTRODUCTION

We thought it might be prudent to offer the reader some essential insights into Bible translation. What is Bible translation? In short, it is the rendering of something written or spoken in one language in words of a different language. However, there are two basic philosophies or methods on how this is to be accomplished. There is the **literal translation**, i.e., lexical or linguistic translation, whose translator or translation committee is determining what English word or phrase in the Hebrew-English or Greek-English lexicon (the technical term for dictionary) corresponds best to the original language word. For example, the Greek word *phronema* can be translated differently as the corresponding English terms are "mind" or "mindset." Therefore, the American Standard Version (ASV), English Standard Version (ESV), and New American Standard Bible (NASB) render *phronema* in Romans 8:27 as "he who searches hearts knows what is the **mind** of the

Spirit." However, the Lexham English Bible (LEB) and the Holman Christian Standard Bible (HCSB) render *phronema* as "the one who searches our hearts knows what the **mindset** of the Spirit is" and "He who searches the hearts knows the Spirit's mind-set" respectively. Both of these renderings are literal.

The literal translation committee is focused on the original language term, with the goal of determining which English word(s) in the lexicon correspond best. The other translation method is known as the **dynamic or functional equivalent** method (Defined below). Their committee is interested in the reader, and the end goal is to take the corresponding English term and find the sense of what is meant, which replaces the literal rendering. Therefore, the Common English Bible (CEB) and the New Life Version (NLV) render *phronema* in Romans 8:27 as "knows how the Spirit **thinks**,"[2] while the Easy to Read Version (ERV) and the New Living Translation (NLT) render it, "understands what the Spirit is **saying**." Below is phronema in Romans 8:6-7 in three literal translations, followed by three dynamic equivalents. The sense of phronema is "what one has in the mind, the thought" (the content of the process expressed in phroneo, "to have in mind, to think"); or "an object of thought" (Vine 1996, Volume 2, Page 409) Logos Bible Software has "**mindset** n. – a habitual or characteristic mental attitude that determines how you will interpret and respond to situations." (Bible Sense Lexicon)

---

[2] It should be admitted that "thinking" is actually a literal rendering of *phronema*, but the more literal of the three would be "mind" and "mindset."

Romans 8:6-7 English Standard Version (ESV)	Romans 8:6-7 New American Standard Bible (NASB)	Romans 8:6-7 Updated American Standard Version (UASV)
[6] For to set the **mind** on the flesh is death, but to set the **mind** on the Spirit is life and peace. [7] For the **mind** that is set on the flesh is hostile to God, for it does not submit to God's law; indeed, it cannot.	[6] For the **mind set** on the flesh is death, but the **mind set** on the Spirit is life and peace, [7] because the **mind set** on the flesh is hostile toward God; for it does not subject itself to the law of God, for it is not even able *to do so*,	[6] For setting the **mind** on the flesh is death, but setting the mind on the spirit is life and peace [7] because setting the **mind** on the flesh means enmity toward God, for it is not subjected to the law of God, for it is not even able to do so
Romans 8:6-7 Common English Bible (CEB)	Romans 8:6-7 Easy-to-Read Version (ERV)	Romans 8:6-7 New Century Version (NCV)
[6] The **attitude** that comes from selfishness leads to death, but the **attitude** that comes from the Spirit leads	[6] If your **thinking** is controlled by your sinful self, there is spiritual death. But if your **thinking** is controlled by the Spirit, there is life and peace. [7] Why is this true?	[6] If people's **thinking** is controlled by the sinful self, there is death. But if their **thinking** is controlled by the Spirit, there is life and peace. [7] When

to life and peace. [7] So the **attitude** that comes from selfishness is hostile to God. It doesn't submit to God's Law, because it can't.	Because anyone whose **thinking** is controlled by their sinful self is against God. They refuse to obey God's law. And really they are not able to obey it.	people's **thinking** is controlled by the sinful self, they are against God, because they refuse to obey God's law and really are not even able to obey God's law.

Glossary of Technical Terms

Time is in one direction and cannot be repeated. B.C.E. means "before the Common Era," which is more accurate than B.C. ("before Christ"). C.E. denotes "Common Era," often called A.D., for *anno Domini,* meaning "in the year of our Lord." It should be noted that the Romans did not have a zero, so time goes from 1 B.C.E. to 1 C.E.

4026 ... 1000 ... 760 ... 406 ... ◀B.C.E. | C.E.▶ 29 ... 33 ... 36 ... 100

Original Language (OL) is the Hebrew and Aramaic for the Old Testament and Greek for the New Testament.

Source Language (SL) is the language of which a translation is being produced in another. Therefore, if one is translating from Hebrew into English, then Hebrew is the SL.

Receptor Language (RL) is just the opposite; it is the language of which the translation is being produced. Therefore, if one is translating from Greek into English, then English is the RL.

As you can see from the above, the terms Source and Receptor Language have the acronym SL and RL respectively. In addition, keep in mind that the text that the translator is rendering into another language is the source text. Please do not confuse the Source Language with the Original Language. True, the Source Language can be the Original Language of say Hebrew or Greek. However, if there is a case of a translator making a Chinese translation of the New Testament, but has chosen to make it from English, the Source Language would be English. The Original Language of the Old Testament is Hebrew, and the New Testament is Greek.

Dynamic Equivalent (DE) is taking the meaning of the original language text in the receptor language of say English and focusing on the sense of the word. For example at Exodus 35:21, the English Standard Version (ESV) literally reads "And they came, everyone whose **heart** stirred him," while the Common English Bible (CEB) committee deemed the figurative use of the "heart" as too difficult, so they rendered it, "Everyone who was excited and eager." The objective of the dynamic equivalent is to translate meaning not words.

Dynamic Equivalence is a method of translation, which is also known as a *sense-for-sense* or *thought-for-thought* translation, whose objective is to translate the meaning of phrases or whole sentences. The objective is to take technical terms, idiomatic expressions, figurative language, and so on, and render them In easy to understand terms that they feel reflect the sense of the OL terms.

Functional Equivalence (FE) is a method of translation that goes beyond the corresponding English word or phrase of the original language, with what is known as a functional equivalent. Again, when the literal rendering is determined to be too difficult for the modern-day reader, the committee will like for a word or phrase that they feel captures the sense of what was meant. For example, the literal NASB at Proverbs 4:15 reads "Drink water from your own cistern," while the functional equivalents ERV reads, "Now, about sex and marriage," and the NCV reads, "Be faithful to your own wife." The FE is attempting to explain the imagery that is found in the literal Translation.

Formal Equivalence (FE) is a word-for-word translation, where the committee gives the reader the corresponding English word, attempting to follow the same word order as the OL. The emphasis is on the OL and the lexical or linguistic interpretation, as well as the grammatical construction.

Literal Translation (LT) gives you what God said, so there is no concealing this by going beyond into the realms of what a translator interprets the sense of these words.

Target Audience (TA) is the audience that the publisher is focusing on reaching with their translation. Once that target audience has been chosen; then, the committee will have this translation philosophy mindset. For example, the Common English Bible target audience is a seventh-grade reading level, "to make the Bible accessible to a broad range of people; it's written at a comfortable level for over half of all English readers."[3]

Portions of scripture were assigned to each of the 120 translators. Each produced a draft translation which was then reviewed and modified by a co-translator. The resulting text was then sent to one of 77 "reading groups," teams of five to ten non-specialists that read it

------

[3] http://www.commonenglishbible.com/

out loud and noted awkward translations. The rendering, along with suggestions for improvement, was then sent to a readability editor to check style and grammar, followed by a complete review by the editor for that section of the Bible. The text was then put before the entire editorial board which resolved any lingering controversies and ensured consistency throughout the entire Bible translation.[4]

Mark 6:12 Updated American Standard Version (UASV) [12] And they went out and proclaimed that men[5] should repent.	Mark 6:12 Common English Bible (CEB) [12] So they went out and proclaimed that people should change their hearts and lives.
Romans 12:2 Updated American Standard Version (UASV) [2] And do not be conformed to this world, but be transformed by the renewing of your mind, so that you may prove what the will of God is, that which is good and acceptable[6] and perfect.	Romans 12:2 Common English Bible (CEB) Don't be conformed to the patterns of this world, but be transformed by the renewing of your minds so that you can figure out what God's will is--what is good and pleasing and mature.

---

[4] http://en.wikipedia.org/wiki/Common_English_Bible
[5] I.e., means both men and women
[6] Or *well-pleasing*

The Search for the Best Translation

It is a daunting task for the new Bible student to walk into a Christian bookstore to purchase a Bible. Immediately, he is met with shelves upon shelves of more than 100 different English translation choices: NIV, TNIV, ESV, NASB, UASV, NRSV, CEV, HCSB, NLT, and on and on. He is even further bewildered when he realizes that there are different formats within each translation: a standard format, a reference Bible, a study Bible, a life application Bible, an archaeology Bible, to name just a few. He further notices that some translations claim to be literal (word-for-word) while others claim to be dynamic or functional equivalent (thought for thought), which has only served to increase his confusion.

God has chosen to convey an essential message to the human family, one that is a matter of life and death. In the Bible of 66 smaller books, we find God's will and purpose for us, as well as what role we need to play to receive the gift of life. Sir Matthew Hale, Lord Chief Justice of England, once said, "The Bible is the only source of all Christian truth; the only rule for the Christian life; the only book that unfolds to us the realities of eternity." (Edwards 1908, p. 40)

If we are to know God, it only makes sense that we must know and understand his Word, the Bible. Jesus Christ makes this all too clear to us when he said in prayer to his Father: "This is eternal life: that they may know You, the only true God, and the One You have sent, Jesus Christ." (John 17:3, HCSB) Here we see that "eternal life" is closely related to our knowing (having a relationship with) God and his Son, Jesus Christ. It is the apostle John who answers the why: "And the world with its lust is passing away, but the one who does God's will remain forever." 1 John 2:17, ESV.

In order to know "the will of God," we must recognize that the Bible is our only guide in this matter. Each Christian should "be filled with the knowledge [lit., accurate or full knowledge] of his will in all spiritual wisdom and understanding, to walk worthily of the Lord unto all pleasing, bearing fruit in every good work, and increasing in the knowledge [lit., accurate or full knowledge] of God." (Col. 1:9, 10, NASB) Is it possible to "walk worthily" of God without fully knowing his will? Is it possible to know his will without first understanding the Bible?

Psalm 119:165 Updated American Standard Version (UASV)

165 Abundant peace belongs to those loving your law,
    And for them, there is no stumbling-block.

At times, it must be difficult for us to contemplate the idea of finding any measure of peace in the world we now know. It is our love for God's law and the application of that law, which will give us a righteous standing before our Creator (being justified in his eyes) and a measure of peace and happiness now. Thus, the incentive to know our Bible is far greater than one might have thought, meaning we are seeking approval in God's eyes as well as peace and happiness and the hope of a future everlasting life.

Looking Behind the Curtain

Have you ever wondered how the actual translation process works? Why is the same Hebrew Old Testament or Greek New Testament word translated differently in the same translation, and even interpreted in others? Christians, who have never worked in the field of translation, have long thought that words are codes. In other words, the translator has the Hebrew or Greek text on one side, to which he simply plugs in an English word for each Greek word, resulting in the English translation. What we will discover herein is that far more is involved in the translation process.

CHAPTER 1 Bible Translation Is a Hazardous Duty

The Bible has faced opposition from Satan's world since the beginning, from supposed "friend" and foe alike. An innumerable number of faithful followers of God have paid with their lives to bring us the Bible in our language today. Even today, there is much pressure from the so-called Christian community and the scholarly world to be faithful to man as opposed to being faithful to God and the original language text when translating the Bible. The closing chapters will deal with that, for now, let's look at the hazardous duty of Bible translation and the lives of three great men.

Bible translation goes back to 280 to 150 B.C.E., when (seventy-two, according to tradition) translators gave us the Hebrew Old Testament books in Greek. From those days forward, translators have lived very dangerous lives, in trying to bring us the Word of God in the common languages of man. Most times this has been from the religious organizations themselves, who have caused the suffering and death of many translators. There are many good books out there on the history of the Bible, one being by Neil R. Lightfoot, *How We Got the Bible*; another by Bruce M. Metzger, *The Bible In Translation*; As well as *Journey from Texts to Translations, The: The Origin and Development of the Bible*, by Paul Wegner.

The English Bible

The English Bible translation came to us in the late fourteenth century. John Wycliffe (c. 1328 – December 31, 1384), is the one credited with the handwritten translation. However, it was not rendered from the original language texts of Hebrew and Greek, but from the Latin Vulgate. Therefore, it was a translation of a translation. Exactly how much of the translation Wycliffe completed before his death in 1384 is unknown. However, what we do know is that there was strong opposition to his work. Both Wycliffe and those helping received bitter hatred from the religious leaders of his day. If it were not for his influence, he would have been martyred like many others.

However, the story of Wycliffe does not end with his death. The Church leadership continued to oppose the copying of the Wycliffe translation. Some 24-years after Wycliffe's death, in 1408, a Church council met in Oxford at the direction of Archbishop Arundel, prohibiting the use of the Holy Scriptures in English. This ban by the clergy was not going to stand up as the people wanted to have a copy of the only English translation available to them. We have evidence of such, as we possess today nearly 200 copies of the Wycliffe translation, many that were made after 1420. John Wycliffe was so despised that these religious leaders had his bones dug up in 1428 to be burned, with the ashes to be cast into the river Swift.

William Tyndale

It would not be until the sixteenth century that we would see a translation that was rendered from the original language texts of Hebrew and Greek. It would be the William Tyndale, who would bring us our first printed English translation. Thinking that he could acquire the backing of Bishop Cuthbert Tunstall, Tyndale went to London. However, he was unsuccessful in getting the bishop's support.

While still in London, Tyndale came to the realization that there would be no translation with the current attitude of the religious leaders in England. Therefore, in 1524 he headed for Germany. Once in Cologne, the translation of the New Testament got underway. However, the magistrates of Cologne were none too happy about this news as it reached them. Thus, they put a stop to the work. This forced Tyndale to move on to Worms; there, the printing of the New Testament was finally completed. In time, translations of this New Testament were flooding England. Meanwhile, back in Worms, Tyndale continued his revision work on the translation.

Needless to say, the English church authorities were beside themselves with rage. On May 4, 1530, copies of Tyndale's translation were burned at St. Paul's Cross in London. At the end of May, there was a royal decree backed by the church authorities, which listed the translation of Tyndale among wicked books and stated, "Detest them, abhor them; keep them not in your hands, deliver them to the superiors such as call for them." For those that would think of ignoring the decree, it continued, "The prelates of the church, having the care and charge of your souls, ought to compel you, and your prince to punish and correct you." There was no effort spared in attempts at destroying the translations in England.

One of the reasons for such great hatred on the part of the religious leaders was Tyndale's choice renderings of some terms. For instance, he chose to use "congregation" over "church;" "overseer" instead of "bishop;" and "love" in place of "charity." It did not matter to the religious authorities that his choice of words was more accurate as to the original language terms. Even still, Tyndale had said he would correct anything that was proven inaccurate, or that could be translated more clearly. The fact of the matter was that the religious authorities knew that these renderings affected the power of the church, giving the power back to the people.

In time, Tyndale's efforts were to come to a close, as a man named Phillips pretended to be his friend and then betrayed him like Judas had done Christ. Tyndale was arrested and imprisoned in the castle of Vilvorde, near Brussels. In September of 1536, he was executed by being strangling and burned.

The man, William Tyndale, a great scholar, set the foundation of translation from the 1611 King James Version, which was 90 percent Tyndale up unto the 2001 English Standard Version. Tyndale knowing that day-in-and-day-out, his life was at risk, but he sought to bring to the English world, the Word of God, and not for glory or honor, but for the love of God and neighbor. There are dozens of men and women, who have suffered martyrdom to bring us God's Word. Truly, the Bible translator has taken on a very dangerous task.

1 Timothy 2:3-4 Updated American Standard Version (UASV)

[3] his is good, and it is acceptable in the sight of God our Savior, [4] who desires all men to be saved and to come to an accurate knowledge[7] of truth.

---

[7]   *Epignosis* is a   strengthened   or   intensified   form of *gnosis* (*epi*, meaning "additional"), meaning, "true," "real," "full," "complete" or "accurate," depending upon the context. Paul and Peter alone use *epignosis.*

The Wycliffe Bible – The Word of Our God Endures Forever

While the Wycliffe Bible is not the first English Bible, it is the first complete English Bible. It came to us through the efforts and influence of John Wycliffe (c. 1330-1384), a Catholic priest and a professor of theology at Oxford, England, called the "morning star of the Reformation" because of the religious principles that he developed through his investigation of Scripture and witnessed about, a great risk to himself. In his treatise of 1378, De Potestate Papae ("Concerning the Authority of the Pope"), Wycliffe was above all open and candid when it came to the church's disregard in teaching the Bible, the timeless "exemplar" of the Christian religion, was the single standard of doctrine, to which no church authority might legitimately add, and that the authority of the pope was unreliable in Scripture.

Wycliffe once declared: "Would to God that every parish church in this land had a good Bible and good expositions on the gospel, and that the priests studied them well, and taught truly the gospel and God's commands to the people!"[8] Wycliffe viewed the Bible as the Word of God, penned to every person. Therefore, he felt personally obligated to render the Scriptures in a translation that the layperson-churchgoer would have access to its truths. Wycliffe was mindful of the mistreatments in the church, which he wrote and preached against, such as bribery in the monastic orders, papal taxation, the doctrine of transubstantiation (the claim that the bread and wine used in the Mass literally change into the body and blood of Jesus Christ), the confession, and church involvement in everyday life. Wycliffe had influential enemies who were finally able to bring him to trial for heresy. Twenty-four theses from his writings and sermons were condemned as heretical or erroneous at a synod held at Blackfriars, London, on May 21, 1382.

It is uncertain whether Wycliffe himself actually worked directly on the translation that bears his name. He died in peace on the last day of 1384 at Lutterworth. However, it is his translation, and rightfully bears his name, the Wycliffe Bible, for if it were not for his inspiration and influence, the translation would have never gotten done. To this end, Wycliffe, in the last years of his life, embarked on the task of translating the Latin Vulgate Bible into English, with the help of his associates, John Purvey and Nicholas of Hereford, two complete versions of the Scriptures were produced. The 1382 version was an extremely literal translation, following the Latin word for word, even violating the English word order. The 1388 version was less literal and more in line the English idiom of his time. Because the translation was made from the Latin Vulgate text, it also included the Old Testament apocryphal and deuterocanonical books.

---

[8] Writings of the Reverend and learned John Wickliff - Page 125

Principles of Bible Translation

Purvey set down some principles of Bible translation:

First, it is to be known that the best translating out of Latin into English is to translate after the sentence and not only after the words, so the sentence be as open or opener, in English as in Latin, and go not far from the letter; and if the letter may not be followed in the translating, let the sentence be ever whole and open, for the words ought to serve the intent and sentence, or else the words be superfluous or false.[9]

Some have been so bold as to use this statement, to suggest that Wycliffe and his associates supported some dynamic equivalent translation philosophy.[10] Well, this certainly could not be further from the truth.

Furthermore, since the charge of naivete is in part an attempt to marginalize adherents of essentially literal translation as an inconsequential segment of the English translation scene, it is important to set the record straight in this regard. Even though new English translations have been dominated by dynamic equivalence, the English Bibles actually in use have been pretty evenly divided between literal and free translations. And in terms of the history of English Bible translation, dynamic equivalence is almost wholly a modern phenomenon. No major English translation was dominated by

---

[9] F. F. Bruce, *The English Bible: A History of Translations* (New York: Oxford Univ. Press, 1961), 19–20.

[10] Strauss, Mark L.; Scorgie, Glen G.; Voth, Steven M.: *The Challenge of Bible Translation: Communicating God's Word to the World.* Zondervan, p. 201.

dynamic equivalence until the mid-twentieth century, and in this regard appeals to the Wycliffe translation of the fourteenth century and occasional freedoms that Tyndale took are irrelevant to the discourse. If Tyndale gave us anomalies like claiming that Paul sailed from Philippi after the Easter holidays, he also coined words like intercession and atonement in order to express the theological con-tent of the original. In terms of the history of English Bible translation, therefore, essentially literal translation is the dominant tradition, not a lightweight view held by a few ignorant people.[11]

The Council of Constance condemned **John Hus** as a heretic, the Bohemian (Czech), who had been influenced by John Wycliffe. Hus refused to recant and was burned to death at the stake in 1415. The same council also ordered that the bones of Wycliffe be dug up and burned although he had been dead and buried for over 30 years! The Wycliffe Bible was condemned and burned as well. Both assistants of Wycliffe, Purvey, and Nicholas would be jailed. They were tortured until they recanted their teachings. Then, in 1428, an outlandish and appalling event occurred. Because Pope Martin V insisted, the grave of John Wycliffe was broken open in accordance with the decree of the Council of Constance made 14 years earlier. His remains were dug up and burned, and the ashes were taken down to the little river Swift a short distance away. However, as the ashes of Wycliffe were carried far and wide by the river, so too was his message throughout the next few centuries.

---

[11] Grudem, Wayne; Packer, J. I.: *Translating Truth: The Case for Essentially Literal Bible Translation.* Good News Publishers/Crossway Books, p. 63.

In 1407 the synod of clergy called in Oxford, England, by Archbishop Thomas Arundel explicitly prohibited the translating of the Bible into English or any other modern tongue.[12] In 1431, also in England, Bishop Stafford of Wells banned the translating of the Bible into English and the possessing of such translations.[13] In spite of this misplaced religious fervor, about 180 copies of the Wycliffe Bible in whole or in part have survived, largely dating prior to 1450. Of these, there are 15 copies of the Old Testament and 18 copies of the New Testament, which are of the 1382 more literal version. Many speak of the influence that Martin Luther's version had on the German language, yet the Wycliffe Bible had no less of an effect on the English people and the English language.

The death of John Wycliffe caused great elation amongst his adversaries. They would no longer be inundated by the difficulties that his teachings had brought about. They would be able to rebuild their grasp over the people. Wycliffe's writings and his Bible translation into English could be destroyed and be out of sight and thus out of mind. Although that may have been their expectation, it did not happen the way that they had hoped. Wycliffe's followers, the Lollards, were more resolute than ever to keep his work alive. Wycliffe's writings and portions of the Bible were circulated all over England by a group of preachers frequently referred to as "Poor Priests" for the reason that they went about in simple clothing, barefoot, and without material belongings. They were also mockingly called Lollards, from the Middle Dutch word Lollaerd, or "one who

---

[12] The Lollard Bible and Other Medieval Biblical Versions, by Margaret Deanesly, 1920, p. 24.

[13] The Lollard Bible, p. 227.

mumbles prayers or hymns."[14] The survival of so many Wycliffe Bibles in the face of such opposition is evidence of the persistence and effectiveness of the courageous Bible preachers: the Lollards![15]

Bruce Metzger informs us in his *The Bible in Translation* that, "during the first half of the fifteenth century, some copies of this version were augmented by the inclusion following Colossians of the spurious Letter of Paul to the Laodicean's. In Colossians 4:16, Paul directs the Colossians, after they have read his letter to them, to pass it on to the church of Laodicea and to see that they, in turn, have an opportunity to "read also the letter from Laodicea." Although no such letter occurs in the New Testament, before the end of the fourth century someone forged such a composition in Paul's name. This inauthentic letter circulated in Latin for many centuries and sometimes was included in manuscripts of the Latin Vulgate."[16]

---

[14] Inc Merriam-Webster, Merriam-Webster's Collegiate Dictionary., Eleventh ed. (Springfield, Mass.: Merriam-Webster, Inc., 2003).

[15] The complete Wycliffe Bible did not appear in a printed edition of until 1850, when Josiah Forshall and Frederic Madden distributed the earlier and the later versions, printed side by side in four volumes (Oxford University Press).

[16] Bruce Metzger. The Bible in Translation, Ancient and English Versions (p. 58).

The Life and Martyrdom of Bible Translator John Hus (1369-1415)

In the first century of our common era, the first martyr gave his life because of his stance for God, Stephen. (Acts 7:54-6) These early disciples of Christ had been given a commission that all Christians are expected to carry out:

Matthew 24:14: Updated American Standard Version (UASV)

[14] And this gospel of the kingdom will be **proclaimed in all the inhabited earth**[17] as a testimony to all the nations, and then the end will come.

Matthew 28:19-20 Updated American Standard Version (UASV)

[19] Go therefore and **make disciples** of all the nations, baptizing them in the name of the Father and the Son and the Holy Spirit, [20] **teaching** them to observe all that I commanded you; and look, I am with you always, even to the end of the age."

---

[17] Or *in the whole world*

Acts 1:8 Updated American Standard Version (UASV)

8 But you will receive power when the Holy Spirit has come upon you; and you will **be my witnesses** in both Jerusalem and in all Judea and Samaria, and **to the end of the earth.**"

Stephen is seized, gives fearless witness, and dies a martyr for daring to bear witness about Christ. James died about 44 C.E. Herod Agrippa I had him executed with the sword. He was the first of the 12 Apostles to die as a martyr. (Ac 12:1-3) The rest of the book of Acts encompasses an unforgettable record of the judgments, imprisonment, and maltreatment, harassment, and downright oppression endured by faithful ones like Peter, and the Apostle Paul, the former persecutor turned apostle, who suffered martyrdom at the hands of Roman Emperor Nero about 65 C.E. – 2 Corinthians 11:23-27; 2 Timothy 4:6-8.

The Apostles Arrested and Freed

Acts 5:17-18 Updated American Standard Version (UASV)

17 But the high priest rose up and all those who were with him (that is, the party of the Sadducees), and they were filled with jealousy. 18 And they laid hands on the apostles and put them in the public prison.

The Angel of the Lord

Acts 5:19-21 Updated American Standard Version (UASV)

19 But during the night an angel of the Lord opened the doors of the prison and led them out and said, 20 "Go and stand in the temple and speak to the people all the

words of this Life." [21] And when they heard this, they entered into the temple about daybreak, and began to teach. Now when the high priest came, and they that were with him, and called the council together, and all the senate of the sons of Israel, and sent to the prison house to have them brought.

The Astonishment of the Jailers

Acts 5:22-26 Updated American Standard Version (UASV)

[22] But the officers who came did not find them in the prison; and they returned and reported, [23] saying, "We found the prison locked with all security and the guards standing at the doors, but when we opened them, we found no one inside." [24] Now when the captain of the temple and the chief priests heard these words, they were greatly perplexed about them, wondering what would come of this. [25] And someone came and told them, "Look! The men whom you put in prison are standing in the temple and teaching the people." [26] Then the captain with the officers went and brought them, but not by force, for they were afraid of being stoned by the people.

The Accusation by the Sanhedrin

Acts 5:27-28 Updated American Standard Version (UASV)

[27] And when they had brought them, they set them before the council. And the high priest questioned them, [28] saying, "We strictly charged you not to teach in this name, yet here you have filled Jerusalem with your teaching, and you intend to bring this man's blood upon us."

The Answer by the Apostles

Acts 5:29-32 Updated American Standard Version (UASV)

29 But Peter and the apostles answered, **"We must obey God rather than men.** 30 The God of our fathers raised Jesus, whom you killed by hanging him on a tree.[18] 31 God exalted this one as Leader and Savior to his right hand, to give repentance to Israel and forgiveness of sins. 32 And we are witnesses to these things, and so is the Holy Spirit, whom God has given to those who obey him."

Ever since that unforgettable first-century, many have boldly followed in the footsteps of Jesus and those first martyrs. Those first-century Christian martyrs stood their ground against the religious leaders of their day, who did not want to hear the truth, and would execute anyone try to share the good news of the kingdom. (Matthew 23:13) This appendix is featuring just such a person, one who stood in the face of a very powerful religious system and refused to back down. John Hus (1371-1415) used those very same words of the Apostle Peter when he was ordered not to preach in his fellow Bohemians. He accepted the supreme authority of God and His Word at a time when virtually everyone else viewed the pope and the church as supreme. How did he come to take this stand?

---

[18] **Wood:** (Gr. *xulon*) simply means wood or anything made of wood and, of course, it can be used to refer to a tree.

The Early Life and Bible Teachings of John Hus

The mother of John Hus was a widow and a peasant, which means that the family would have struggled for the simple necessities of like, let alone an education. Like Martin Luther, he chose to sing and perform services in churches to earn a living for the family. Initially, his desire to consider being of the clergy was because of their lifestyle that was free from the stresses of the day. As a student at the University of Prague Hus did not distinguish himself, as he was not a brilliant young man by any means. In 1393, he received his Bachelor of Arts, in 1394 Bachelor of Theology, and in 1396 Master of Arts. In around 1400, he was able to become an ordained priest; in 1401, he became dean of the philosophical faculty, and in the following year rector of the university. In addition, in 1402, he was chosen to preach at the Bethlehem Church in Prague, where he preached in the Czech language.

Throughout this period, there was much conflict between the Germans and the Czechs in the university. Hus would become a defender of the Czech cause, all the while his influence was growing because his preaching was becoming all the more powerful. Since 1382, the writings of the English Morning Star of Reformers, John Wycliffe had been pouring into Bohemia, and Hus had been taking them in all through his student days, especially the work On Truth of Holy Scripture, which he obtained in 1407. All the while, there had been a discontent and debate over many mistreatments involving the Roman Catholic Church. While many believe that the Bohemian Reformation only came about because of the stirrings in England, this just is not the case; they ran parallel to each other.

One line of opposition came from Archbishop Zbynek of Prague, who took exception to Hus' preaching. To get even with Hus, Zbynek publicly burned the writings of Wycliffe in 1410. Another tactic to shut Hus out was to forbid preaching except in recognized churches, which would exclude the Bethlehem Chapel where Hus presided. Well, like any good reformer, Hus chose to disobey the archbishop's prohibition, stating that he had to "obey God rather than men in things which are necessary for salvation." Hus chose rather to take his case to the pope but was excommunicated by the archbishop for his efforts. However, Hus did not falter, finding that his better understanding had honed his conscience and made it more sensitive to the Word of God. He clearly stated, "Man may lie, but God lies not," stressing the Apostle Paul's words to the Romans. (Romans 3:4) King Wenceslas defended Hus' reform movement, and eventually, Zbynek took flight out of the country, dying shortly thereafter.

Hostility and opposition were soon Hus' bedfellow yet again. He condemned a movement against the king of Naples and uncovered the sale of indulgences for it, therefore ruining the priests' income. Indulgences were letters of pardon issued by the pope for sins, which permitted a person to get relief from temporal punishment for the payment of money. To not bring any problems to the city of Prague, he fled into the country. While in exile, he wrote the work On Simony, which made the folks well aware of the clergy's love of money, as well as their cohorts the secular authorities, who supported them as they soaked the poor of all they had. As was true of most reformers, in difficult times, they would depend on God's Word to lead the way, so Hus defended his position with, "Every faithful Christian should be so minded as not to hold anything contrary to the Holy Scriptures."

Hus shortly thereafter wrote an exposition entitled De Ecclesia (On the Church). Within the paper, he expressed a number of suggestions, one of which was the fact "That Peter never was, and is not, the head of the Church." Hus had determined from his exposition of Matthew 16:15-18 that it was not Peter, who was the foundation and head of the church; it was Jesus Christ, who filled that position. For Hus, the real authority belongs to the law of Christ, which was found in the Word of God, not man.

The Council of Constance

The rivalry had grown to the point where the Catholic Church could no longer sit by while Hus buried them in publication after publication, exposing their wrongdoing. They sent for him to come and answer for his views before the Council of Constance, held from 1414 to 1418 near Lake Constance. On December 4, 1414, the pope had delegated a committee of three bishops with an initial inquiry against Hus. The witnesses for the prosecution had their opportunity to speak, but Hus was not allowed a supporter for his defense. He continued to stand fast against the authority of the pope.

The council at one point asked Hus to withdraw his teachings, and he responded that he would if they could prove him wrong with Scripture, in accordance with 2 Timothy 3:14-16. Hus allowed his Christian conscience to lead the way and knew that he would never live with himself if he offered some vague retraction that might save face and save his life. He clearly stated, "My wish always has been that better doctrine be proved to me out of Scripture, and then I would be most ready to recant." He challenged the council to have their least member to show him from God's Word where he erred. They were not so inclined and condemned him as a heretic instead and him back to prison without anything being discussed from the Bible.

The condemnation of Hus took place on July 6, 1415; he was officially condemned in the cathedral of Constance. The bishop of Lodi delivered a discourse on the duty of eliminating heresy; then some theses of Hus and Wycliffe and a report of his trial were read. Hus objected several times loudly, and when his appeal to Christ was rejected as a condemnable heresy, he exclaimed, "O God and Lord, now the council condemns even thine own act and thine own law as heresy since thou thyself didst lay thy cause before thy Father as the just judge, as an example for us, whenever we are sorely oppressed."

John Hus had his priesthood publicly stripped from him, as well as having his writings burned in the churchyard. At some point, he was led out into a field and burned at the stake.

The Accomplishments of John Hus

The accomplishments of John Hus at reform were 100 years before the start of the official Reformation, which was started by Martin Lither in 1517. John Hus and John Wycliffe were pioneers in opposing the pope and having their only true guide be that of the authority of Scripture. Hus helped to begin the commencement of the freedom of individuals, to allow their conscience to decide what is Scriptural and what is not.

In the early 1500s, Martin Luther was making a similar name for himself, as he was considered a Hussite. Obviously, we see Hus in his words, "Unless I am convicted by Scripture and plain reason—I do not accept the authority of popes and councils, for they have contradicted each other—my conscience is captive to the Word of God." Perhaps that is why he said: "We are all Hussites without knowing it."

John Hus, John Wycliffe, Martin Luther, and William Tyndale were the foundation of this return to Scripture, something that took the Reformation back to being like first-century Christianity. Of course, these ones did, not easily set the darkness of the period between the end of the Roman Empire in the fifth century and the early fifteenth-century, aside, as they were not able to shake off all the doctrines of tradition, but they established quite a few. Together, they reestablished the doctrine of *sola scriptura*, or Scripture alone, which means that Scripture, not popes or church councils, establishes all doctrinal matters. They returned to the Lord Jesus Christ, and early Christians enlightened view on this matter. – John 17:17; 18:37.

There is a battle that has been underway over the last 150-years between liberal Christianity and conservative Christianity, and it all boils down to the Bible. The liberal movement does not see the Bible as the Word of God, but instead, sees it as the word of men, filled with errors and contradictions, as well as myths and legends. The true conservative movement, on the other hand, sees the Bible as the Word of God, inspired and fully inerrant, the foundation of all they believe to be true.

Sadly, the liberal scholarship movement is at about 80 percent, with the conservative being around 20 percent. We are in a battle for the survival of the faith, and we too must take the same stand as that of John Hus, who echoed the words of the apostles, "We must obey God as ruler rather than men." – Acts 5:29.

The Betrayal and Martyrdom of the Translator William Tyndale

We have a young man, who had been on the run from the Catholic church for many years, all the while working as a printer and a translator of the English Bible. Many times, there was a pounding at the door, only to find that this translator and his apprentice has left moments earlier. The Catholic Church viewed the Bible in the language of the common people as illegal literature,

41

because the people were too illiterate to understand the Word of God. The Bible had been locked up in the dead language of Latin for almost a thousand years. Who was the translator? He was William Tyndale, i.e., "God's Outlaw," who had been pursued by the false friend of the Catholic Church, as though he were the worst criminal on the planet in the early 16th-century. While King James is credited with the most popular Bible that has ever been published, it was actually William Tyndale who should be credited, because the 1611 King James Version was 97 percent Tyndale's English translation. The Word of God has had many enemies since the first book, Genesis, was published, some 3,500 years ago.

The clergy was extremely bitterly opposed to Tyndale's translation. Why? The Latin *Vulgate* had a tendency of veiling the sacred text for 500 years, while Tyndale's translation from the original Greek conveyed the Bible's message in clear language to the people of England for the first time. For instance, Tyndale chose to translate the Greek word *agape* as "love" instead of "charity" in 1 Corinthians chapter 13. He rendered the Greek word ecclesia as "congregation" as opposed to "church" so as to emphasize worshipers, rather than church buildings. This took the power back from the church and gave it to the people. The last in a series of unpleasant events that finally made the Catholic Church feel that they could not continue to accept William Tyndale's translation, not his existence was when he replaced "priest" with "elder" and used "repent" rather than "do penance." Tyndale in so doing stripped the clergy of their assumed priestly powers. David Daniell says in this regard: "Catholic revisionists are not there; **Purgatory is not there; there is no aural confession and penance. Two supports of the Church's wealth and power collapsed.** Instead, there was simply individual faith in Christ as Saviour, found in Scripture." (*William Tyndale—A Biography*, 58) That was the difficulty that Tyndale's translation place on the Catholic Church, and modern-day scholarship fully endorse the correctness of his word choices.

Between 1526 and 1528, Tyndale moved to Antwerp. It was here that he felt a little safe among the English merchants. There he wrote *The Parable of the Wicked Mammon, The Obedience of a Christian Man,* and *The Practice of Prelates.* Tyndale never abandoned his translation work. Another step toward the accuracy of Tyndale's translation was the fact that he was the first to use God's personal name, Jehovah, in an English translation of the Hebrew Old Testament Scriptures. The divine name appears over 20 times. It would also be used 4 times in the 1611 King James Version as well.

Eventually, the Englishman Henry Phillips cunningly inveigled himself into Tyndale's confidences. "Henry Phillips was the third and last son in the family ... Phillips threw himself into the company of the English merchants, and by his silver tongue and golden hand won the confidence of all except Thomas Poyntz, the man who gave Tyndale safe lodging in Antwerp. It was not long before Tyndale, who was frequently invited to dine with the merchants, found himself in the same company, and Henry Phillips had come face to face with his prey. Unsuspecting, the reformer felt attracted to the easy manner and eloquent speech of the young student lawyer, and before long he invited him to the Poyntzes' home. There he dined, admired Tyndale's small library, warmly commended his labors, and talked easily of the affairs in England and the need for reform. He even stayed overnight. Thomas Poyntz had misgivings about the relative stranger, but when Tyndale assured him of the man's Lutheran sympathies, he put his doubts aside. This was the greatest mistake Tyndale ever made."[19] As a result,

---

[19] Retrieved Monday, August 5, 2019

in 1535, Tyndale was betrayed and taken to Vilvorde Castle, which was six miles north of Brussels. There he was imprisoned for sixteen months.

> The castle of Vilvoorde had been erected in 1374 by one of the dukes of Brabant, and since it was modeled upon the infamous Bastille, built in Paris at about the same time, its moat, seven towers, three drawbridges and massive walls made it an impregnable prison. The castle was used as the state prison for the Low Countries, and Tyndale was thrown into one of the foul—smelling, damp dungeons with nothing for company but the lapping moat, the squabbling moorhens outside, and the dripping walls and scurrying rats inside. Here, in his solitary darkness, Tyndale waited for the end.[20]

William Tyndale like others before him and others who would come after him would give his life, so that the people of England could have an accurate Bible translation. He paid the ultimate price, but he also gave us the priceless gift! Dr. Leland Ryken of Wheaton College helps us better appreciate just what we received from Tyndale,

> This essay is a historical study. That may seem anomalous in a journal devoted to current translation issues and practices, so a word of explanation is in order. One of the functions of inquiring into the history of English Bible translation is that it can clarify the essential principles of Bible translation. When the issues are distanced from us in time, we can see some things

---

https://christianhistoryinstitute.org/magazine/article/tyndales-betrayal-and-death

[20] IBID.

more clearly because they are unclouded by contemporary crosswinds.

More important than the clarifying power of distance, though, is the authority that attaches to historical precedents. This authority may or not be completely valid, but it is a fact that in the current debate between rival translation philosophies an appeal to historical precedents is considered important. Both literal translators and dynamic equivalent and colloquial translators probe the past to find examples of their own preferred style of translation.

The Current Debate about William Tyndale

It is obvious that we live in a day of debunking. On the Bible translation scene, advocates of colloquial English Bible translations regularly and rigorously debunk the King James Version. In turn, it has become common for these debunkers to attempt to drive a wedge between the King James Version and William Tyndale's translation work nearly a century earlier.

More specifically, the claim is made that the King James translators spoiled Tyndale by refining his style. Eugene Peterson, the author of The Message, has, of course, led the charge, but he is not alone. Predictably, the claim is made that Tyndale produced a colloquial translation while the King James translation is elegant. Peterson claims that the King James translators "desecrated language upwards" [Eat This Book (Grand Rapids: Eerdmans, 2006), 162].

The most famous statement that Tyndale made about Bible translation, next to his dying prayer that God would open the king of England's eyes, is a comment that he made about wanting the plowboy to know the Bible better than the Catholic priests. I will quote the statement shortly and then analyze it, but as a lead-in to that, I need to note that translators in what I call the "modernizing" camp claim that Tyndale in a single utterance endorsed (1) a colloquial style for an English Bible, (2) an uneducated reader as the assumed audience for an English Bible, and (3) a dynamic equivalent philosophy of translation (buttressed, of course, by a few famous examples from Tyndale's actual translation). My thesis in this article is that Tyndale's plowboy statement has been extravagantly misinterpreted and that none of the three conclusions I listed in the previous sentence is warranted.

Exactly what did Tyndale say?

Tyndale's plowboy statement is recounted in John Foxe's Book of Martyrs. The context of the statement itself disproves the use to which modernizing translators put it. Tyndale had uttered the statement before he had even begun his work of translating the Bible. The occasion of the statement was not Bible translation per se. Instead, the statement occurred as part of the debate about whether the pope or the Bible is the ultimate authority for religious belief and practice.

Upon graduating from Oxford University, Tyndale returned to his native Gloucestershire and assumed the position as a schoolmaster in the Catholic household of Sir John Walsh. Tyndale was an early Reformer whose views brought him into heated debates with the local clergy. Tyndale was appalled at the ignorance of the Catholic clergy. Additionally, he was convinced of the Protestant doctrine of sola scriptura on the question of religious authority. I propose that these two things, the biblical ignorance of the clergy and the question of biblical authority, are the context for Tyndale's statement about the plowboy.

We can hear these two themes of biblical ignorance among the clergy and the authority of Bible in the statement that I now quote:

> There dwelt not far off a certain doctor, that he been chancellor to a bishop, who had been of old, familiar acquaintance with Master Tyndale, and favored him well; unto whom Master Tyndale went and opened his mind upon divers questions of the Scripture: for to him he durst be bold to disclose his heart. Unto whom the doctor said, "Do you not know that the pope is very Antichrist, whom the Scripture speaketh of? But beware what you say; for if you shall be perceived to be of that opinion, it will cost you your life." Not long after, Master Tyndale happened to be in the company of a certain divine, recounted for a learned man, and, in communing and disputing with him, he drove him to that issue, that the said great doctor burst out into these blasphemous words, "We were better to be without God's laws than the pope's." Master Tyndale, hearing this, full of godly zeal, and not bearing that blasphemous saying, replied, "I defy the pope, and all his laws;" and added, "If God spared him life, ere many years he would cause a boy that driveth the plough to know more of the Scripture than he did." The grudge of the priests increasing still more and more against Tyndale, they never ceased barking and rating at him, and laid many things sorely to his charge, saying that he was a heretic.

We should note first what is not going on here. The statement about the plowboy is not a comment about Tyndale's preferred style for an English Bible. It is not a designation of teenage farm boys as a target audience for a niche Bible. In fact, the account does not even mention translation of the Bible into English. Foxe's account makes it clear that the subject of debate at this early stage in Tyndale's career was the question of papal authority vs. scriptural authority. When the priest asserted a strong view of papal authority and denigrated the authority of the Bible, Tyndale responded by making an implied case for the Bible as the authority for Christian belief and conduct. We should not overlook Foxe's follow-up comment about "the grudge of the priests." The plowboy statement is part of a debate with Catholic priests over papal authority, not on the style of an English Bible.

Therefore, what did Tyndale mean in his famous plowboy statement? First, he implicitly asserted the right of the laity to the Bible. The plowboy is a representative of the whole of English society. Tyndale's statement is not a comment about English style but about how widely Tyndale wanted the English Bible to be disseminated in English society. Even the humble working class should have access to the Bible.

Secondly, Tyndale was making a statement about how much of the Bible he wanted the laity to know. His statement, to quote again, is "that he would cause a boy that driveth the plough to know more of the Scripture than [the priest] did." The typical priest knew the snatches of Scripture that were embedded in the liturgy, the mass, and choral music, and he would have known it in Latin.

What I most want to challenge is the view that Tyndale was an ally of what I call modernizing and colloquializing English Bibles that have proliferated since the middle of the twentieth century. Whatever we conclude about Tyndale's preferred style in English translation is something we need to deduce from his actual translation, not from his statement about the plowboy.

Conclusion

Tyndale's plowboy statement is a virtual Rorschach inkblot [interpretation] in which modern translators see what they themselves believe about English Bible translation. In turn, Tyndale is such a towering figure that if one can claim him for one's side in the translation wars, it is, in fact, a victory. I submit that Tyndale's plowboy statement should not be allowed to lend any support whatever to dynamic equivalent and colloquial translations. Exactly where Tyndale stood on questions of essentially literal vs. dynamic equivalence and dignified vs. colloquial style needs to rest on his actual translation of the Bible.

By 1538, King Henry VIII for whatever reason came to order that Bibles be placed in every church in England. While William Tyndale was not given the credit, the translation that was decided upon was essentially his Bible. In this way, Tyndale's translation work was so well-known and cherished that it "determined the fundamental character of most of the subsequent versions" in English. (The Cambridge History of the Bible) As much as 90 percent of the Tyndale translation was transferred directly into the 1611 King James Bible. And so, it was that William Tyndale was martyred (gave his life) for the honor of giving a Bible that could easily be understood to the people of England. What a price he had paid, however; it was a priceless gift! Tyndale with his skills and gift of language had done his work well; he had made the Word of God known to the common people. Tyndale and others before and after him had worked with the shadow of death towering over their heads. However, by delivering the Bible to many people in their native tongue, they opened up before them the possibility, not of death, but of life eternal. As Jesus Christ said in the Tyndale Bible, "This is lyfe eternall that they myght knowe the that only very God and whom thou hast sent Iesus Christ." (John 17:3) May we, therefore, know the value of what we can now hold in our hands and may we diligently study God's Word.

CHAPTER 2 The First View on Translating John 8:58

Historical Setting Kenneth O. Gangel

E. Truth and Reality (8:48–59)

SUPPORTING IDEA: No religious appeal to Abraham can withstand honest exposure. Religious self-righteousness must be abandoned by any who would receive God's grace.

8:48–51. Now the discussion turned ugly. Jesus' opponents had already questioned his proof and family connections; now they said what they had been thinking all along: **you are a Samaritan and demon-possessed.** Few insults could have carried more anger and bitterness in the first century. But Jesus ignored the name calling. He stuck to his basic theme of true discipleship by emphasizing that true disciples keep Jesus' words. The Lord emphasized truth and explained his relationship to the Father. In verse 51 the opening phrase (**I tell you the truth**) translates the two words *amen, amen* which appear in 127 verses of the New Testament.

Some interpreters emphasize the ethnic barriers John had already described in chapter 4. But the context deals not so much with religious practice as it does with rejection of Jesus. This may have been an intentional jab at his roots. We do not see the accusation of being a Samaritan anywhere else in the Bible, but demon-possession appears in John 7:20; 8:52 and 10:20 and in the synoptic Gospels as well (Matt. 9:34; 11:18; 12:24ff.; Mark 3:22ff.).

Let us not lose the message of eternal life in the difficult discussions of this chapter. John maintained this theme because he had heard Jesus speak of it so often. The Son does not glorify himself. The Father glorifies him. Those who trust the Son's word advance the Father's glory and **will never see death.**

8:52–53. The question of who would die and when and how and what would happen after death had occupied Jewish theology for centuries. Suddenly Jesus appeared, talking about life after death in almost casual terms and assuring hearers that acceptance of truth meant that true disciples would never die.

In verse 24 he had warned the religious leaders that they would die in their sins if they did not believe his message. He had been speaking about the Father's presence and returning there. But they saw only the earthly interpretation. Abraham died. The prophets died. Yet this strange Galilean promised a life with no death? Obviously, he must consider himself greater than Abraham and the prophets, an unthinkable arrogance which they diagnosed as demon possession. Do not miss the switch in the key question from "Who are you?" in verse 25 to **Who do you think you are?** in verse 53.

8:54–56. True disciples of Jesus are hated by the world. Jesus had been trying to tell them since the beginning of the discussion that he did not stand alone in witnessing the truth of his message. In fact, it was not his message at all but the message of the Father, the one they claimed as their God. Interpretations of these verses must recognize two different Greek verbs translated by the English word **know** in verse 55. These religious leaders did not know God by experience (*oidao*), but Jesus knew him by personal relationship (*ginosko*). Jesus came to tell them the truth about his relationship with the Father.

The reference to **my day** in verse 56 delineated Christ's birth and time on earth. Some interpreters have narrowed it to the crucifixion and/or resurrection, but such a scenario seems unwarranted here. Tenney connects an Old Testament promise to this statement, linking back to Genesis 12:3. "Although this interpretation is not founded on any specific statement of Scripture, it would mean that Abraham's personal experience at the sacrifice of Isaac could have been an object lesson to him of the coming incarnation, death, and resurrection of the promised Seed (see Gen. 22:1–18; Heb. 11:17–19)" (Tenney, *EBC*, pp. 98–99).

8:57–59. By this time the rejecting skeptics' patience had been bent to the breaking point. This young man (interesting they should say **not yet fifty years old**) had seen Abraham? Jesus' response provided the final blow. Once again he picked up a theme from the Old Testament: "God said to Moses, 'I am who I am. This is what you are to say to the Israelites: "I am has sent me to you" ' " (Exod. 3:14). In this chapter Jesus made himself equal with God, a cornerstone of biblical theology. How did they respond? **They picked up stones to stone him**, but Jesus slipped away **from the temple grounds.**

Borchert has a helpful paragraph on Jesus' claim to be one with the Father: "Extending the present into the past does not compute in most of our minds. It is a confusion to the way we think. But God does not fit into the teacups of our minds. More pertinent for our purposes, however, is the fact that Jesus claimed to be 'I AM' over against Abraham. That claim was a reminder of the claims for God in the Old Testament over against creation (cf. Ps. 90:2; Isa. 42:3–9) and of the self-designation for the comforting God of Isaiah (41:4; 43:3, 13). The claim of Jesus, therefore, was clearly recognized from the Jews' perspective to be a blasphemous statement they could not tolerate" (Borchert, p. 309).[21]

Bible Background Clinton E. Arnold

The Jews' and Jesus' Relationship to Abraham (8:31–59)

Hold to my teaching (8:31). The measure of any disciple is whether or not one holds to the master's teaching (cf. 2 John 9). The perfect follower of a Jewish rabbi was one who had "fully absorbed his master's teaching" and "was drawing on it to spread it abroad" (*b. Yoma* 28a; see also *T. Jos.* 1:3: "I have not gone astray: I continued in the truth of the Lord"; *Gospel of*

---

[21] Kenneth O. Gangel, *John*, vol. 4, Holman New Testament Commentary (Nashville, TN: Broadman & Holman Publishers, 2000), 167–169.

Thomas 19: "If you become my disciples and listen to my words …").

Then you will know the truth, and the truth will set you free (8:32). Judaism held that what made people free was the study of the law. "R. Nehunya b. Ha-Kanah [c. a.d. 70–130] said: 'He that takes upon himself the yoke of the Law, from him shall be taken away the yoke of the kingdom and the yoke of worldly care; but he that throws off the yoke of the Law, upon him shall be laid the yoke of the kingdom and the yoke of worldly care" (*m. 'Abot* 3:5; cf. 6:2; 1QS 4:20–21).

In Greek philosophy, both freedom and truth constituted virtues along with self-restraint, justice, and courage. Philo wrote an entire essay on the Stoic notion that only the wise man is free. The Stoics believed that freedom was acquired by living in accordance with Reason. The Stoic philosopher Epictetus (c. a.d. 50–120), son of a slave woman and for many years a slave himself, devoted his entire life to a passionate quest for freedom and independence. He contended that "freedom by the truth" (to be understood in terms of intellectual emancipation against the background of Epictetus's own slave background) is found by following some great philosopher. Jesus' words would surely have resonated in the minds of John's Greek-speaking audience: One greater than Plato and Aristotle was here.

We are Abraham's descendants (8:33). Several Old Testament passages extol the blessings of descent from Abraham: "O descendants of Abraham his servant, O sons of Jacob, his chosen ones" (Ps. 105:6); "But you, O Israel, my servant, Jacob, whom I have chosen, you descendants of Abraham my friend" (Isa. 41:8). However, even then, physical descent from Abraham was considered insufficient by itself. While both Ishmael and Esau were Abraham's offspring, they were not sons of promise.[246] Thus Paul concluded, "For not all who are descended from Israel are Israel. Nor because they are his descendants are they all Abraham's children" (Rom. 9:6–7).

Descent from Abraham was the Jews' pride and a major source of confidence regarding their salvation (cf. esp. Matt. 3:9 par., including John the Baptist's exhortation).[247] The Jews considered Abraham to be the founder of the worship of God; he recognized the Creator and served him faithfully. Apart from descent from Abraham, it was God's deliverance of the Israelites from slavery in Egypt that was seen to ensure the Jews' freedom: "God brought Israel out of captivity ... from darkness and the shadow of death ... from a yoke of iron to the yoke of the Torah ... from slavery to freedom ... from servitude to redemption" (*Ex. Rab.* 15:11).

REFLECTIONS

FREEDOM IS ONE OF HUMANITY'S most prized possessions. Yet freedom is more than being able to do whatever a person would like to do. Freedom must be founded on truth, including the truth of human sinfulness. Only the one who has faced his or her own sinfulness and acknowledged a need for a Savior—Jesus—can experience true freedom. Sin enslaves even those who deem themselves "free" merely because they enjoy a certain degree of personal or political independence. But those who have trusted in the "Lamb of God, who takes away the sin of the world" have been set free from their bondage to sin.

And have never been slaves of anyone (8:33). Freedom was considered the birthright of every Jew.

God's law laid down that no Jew, however poor, must ever descend to the level of slave: "If one of your countrymen becomes poor among you and sells himself to you, do not make him work as a slave…. Because the Israelites are my servants, whom I brought out of Egypt, they must not be sold as slaves" (Lev. 25:39–42). According to the Talmud, R. Simeon b. Gamaliel, R. Simeon, R. Ishmael, and R. Akiba held that "all Israel are royal children" (*b. Šabb.* 128a; cf. Matt. 8:12: "subjects of the kingdom").

Everyone who sins is a slave to sin (8:34). Jewish ethics viewed human existence as conflict between the evil and good impulses (*yeṣer*, e.g., *m. Ber.* 9:5). The law served to restrain the evil impulse and to help the good impulse prevail. The idea that serious offenses subject humankind to the power of sin is attested in both Jewish intertestamental and rabbinic literature. The second-century b.c. work *Testaments of the Twelve Patriarchs* features the following: "The prince of error blinded me, and I was ignorant—as a human being, as flesh, in my corrupt sins—until I learned of my own weakness after supposing myself to be invincible" (*T. Jud.* 19:4); "Flee from the evil tendency, destroying the devil by your good works. For those who are two-faced are not of God, but they are enslaved to their evil desires, so that they might be pleasing to Beliar and to persons like themselves" (*T. Ash.* 3:2).

Rabbinic Judaism concurred. "Happy is he who is [master] over his transgressions, but his transgressions are not [master] over him." R. Akiba (d. c. a.d. 135) said, "At first it [the evil impulse] is like a spider's web, but eventually it becomes like a ship's rope" (*Gen. Rab.* 22:6). The reality of sin was also acknowledged by the Qumran community (CD 1:8–9: "And they realized their sin and knew that they were guilty men"). Greek philosophy, on the other hand, prized wisdom, self-control, and other virtues. According to the Stoics, only the wise are free; the fool is a slave. Socrates denied that an individual can be called free who is controlled by passions. In the present instance, Yom Kippur, the Day of Atonement, which had just passed, should have served as a reminder that the Jews, too, were sinners.[252]

A slave has no permanent place in the family, but a son belongs to it forever (8:35). Compare the reference to Genesis 21:10 in Galatians 4:30: "The slave woman's son will never share in the inheritance with the free woman's son." In both Palestine and the Hellenistic world, households included slaves as well as sons. For Jewish slaves, this dependent relationship lasted only six years; in the seventh year they must be set free. In the Greco-Roman world, too, slaves were occasionally granted freedom, though this was not formally mandated.

The notion of a "son" being set over God's house "forever" is found in an important messianic text: "I will be his father, and he will be my son.... I will set him over my house and my kingdom forever; his throne will be established forever" (1 Chron. 17:13–14). The special status of sons even with regard to taxation by earthly kings is affirmed by Jesus in Matthew 17:25–26. In Hebrews 3:5–6, Moses and Christ are contrasted in terms of the temporary status of servant and the permanent position of son.

If you were Abraham's children ... then you would do the things Abraham did (8:39). In Genesis 18:1–8, Abraham welcomed divine messengers with eager hospitality. In 12:1–9; 15:1–6; 22:1–19, he displayed obedience to God (though the book of Genesis records less noble instances in Abraham's life as well). The rabbis frequently upheld Abraham as a moral example to be emulated by the Jews: "He in whom are these three things is of the disciples of Abraham our father.... A good eye and a humble spirit and a lowly soul—[they in whom are these] are of the disciples of Abraham our father" (*m. 'Abot* 5:19); "Whoever is merciful to his fellow-men is certainly of the children of our father Abraham, and whosoever is not merciful to his fellow-men is certainly not of the children of our father Abraham" (*b. Beṣa* 32b). In rabbinic literature, a distinction is made between people who act like Abraham and those who act like Balaam (*m. 'Abot* 5:19). Generally, Abraham was believed to have fulfilled the whole Torah even before the law was given.

"You are doing the things your own father does." "We are not illegitimate children" (8:41). "Illegitimate children" translates the literal "have been born of sexual immorality" (*porneia*). The prophets had compared Yahweh's covenant with Israel to a marriage relationship: idolatry amounted to spiritual adultery. The Jews' rebuttal may imply that they considered Jesus' birth illegitimate.[255] The earliest attestation of the Jewish belief that Jesus was born out of *porneia* may be *m. Yeb.* 4:13: "I found a family register in Jerusalem and in it was written, 'Such-a-one is a bastard through [a transgression of the law of] thy neighbour's wife (Lev. 18:20),' confirming the words of R. Joshua."

The only Father we have is God himself (8:41). In 8:39, the Jews had said that Abraham is their father (cf. 8:33, 37). Now they say they have only one father, God. This is entirely in keeping with Old Testament teaching (though not necessarily Jewish practice): "This is what the Lord says: Israel is my firstborn son" (Ex. 4:22). "Is ... the Lord ... not your Father, your Creator, who made you and formed you?" (Deut. 32:6). "But you are our Father, though Abraham does not know us or Israel acknowledge us; you, O Lord, are our Father, our Redeemer from of old" (Isa. 63:16). "Yet, O Lord, you are our Father. We are the clay, you are the potter; we are all the work of your hand" (Isa. 64:8). "I am Israel's father, and Ephraim is my firstborn son" (Jer. 31:9). "Have we not all one Father? Did not one God create us?" (Mal. 2:10).

I came from God (8:42). In pagan religions, the term "come" (*hēkō*) was commonly used for the saving appearance of deity. In Jesus' case, it refers to his divine origin. This is part of John's portrayal of Jesus as coming from God and returning to him (metaphorically depicted in terms of descent and ascent; cf. 16:28).

You belong to your father, the devil.... He was a murderer from the beginning (8:44). The plot to kill Jesus (cf. 8:37, 40) is ultimately inspired by Satan himself (13:2, 27). The phrase "murderer from the beginning" primarily refers to the fall narrative in Genesis 3 rather than the first murder in Genesis 4. It was commonly recognized in Jewish intertestamental literature that death was the result of Satan's initiative: "God created us for incorruption, and made us in the image of his own eternity, but through the devil's envy death entered the world, and those who belong to his company experience it" (Wisd. Sol. 2:23–24; cf. Sir. 25:24; Rom. 5:12).

Still, a reference to Cain, the murderer of Abel, may be secondarily in view (cf. 1 John 3:15). If so, Jesus' comment may imply that the devil is the father of "the Jews" because they want to kill Jesus, their fellow-Jew, just as Cain killed his brother Abel. Other Jewish intertestamental texts refer to those outside the community as "children of destruction" (*Jub.* 15:26), "sons of Beliar" (15:33), or "sons of darkness" (1QS 1:10; 1QM passim). Finally, Antiochus Epiphanes IV, who erected the "abomination of desolation" in the Jewish temple in 167 b.c. and who serves as a type of the Antichrist in biblical literature, is called "murderer and blasphemer" in 2 Macc. 9:28 (see comments on John 10:38).

Not holding to the truth, for there is no truth in him (8:44). "Not holding to the truth" may refer to the fall of Satan (Isa. 14:12?), which preceded the fall narrative in Genesis 3. Parallels are found at Qumran: "The Community council shall be founded on truth ... true witnesses for the judgment and chosen by the will (of God)" (1QS 8:5–6); "they look for you with a double heart, and are not firmly based in your truth" (1QH 12:14).

He is a liar and the father of lies (8:44). See Genesis 2:17; 3:4; and previous comment. In the Scrolls, the opponent of the Teacher of Righteousness is called the "Man of Lies" (1QpHab 2:1–2; 5:11; CD 20:15). The Teacher himself says of the people who want to divert him from his path, "They are sowers of deceit and seers of fraud, they have plotted evil against me ... and are not firmly based in your truth" (1QH 12:9–10, 14).

Can any of you prove me guilty of sin? (8:46). In Isaiah 53:9, it is said regarding the Suffering Servant that there was no "deceit in his mouth." Alluding to this passage, *Testament of Judah* 24:1 speaks of the Star from Jacob, who will arise like the Sun of righteousness, "and in him will be found no sin" (this may be a Christian interpolation). Christ's sinlessness is affirmed by the unanimous testimony of the early church. See also *Gospel of Thomas* 104: "What is the sin that I have committed, or wherein have I been defeated?"

You are a Samaritan and demon-possessed (8:48). The Jews' riposte challenges Jesus' *paternity* in return: If he says the Jews are of their "father the devil" (8:44), he will be charged with having been birthed by a Samaritan! The label *Samaritan* may also imply the charge of apostasy. Like the Samaritans, Jesus calls into question the legitimacy of the Jews' worship. Finally, "Samaritan" may intimate that Jesus' *miracles are due to demonic influence or magic.* In the Babylonian Talmud, a person who learned Scripture and the Mishnah but did not study with a rabbi is described by one teacher as belonging to "the people of the land," by another as a Samaritan, and by a third as a magician.[263]

I honor my Father and you dishonor me (8:49). Christ's calm, non-retaliatory response evokes reminiscences of Isaiah's Suffering Servant (cf. 1 Peter 2:23 alluding to Isa. 53:7). According to Jewish law, rejection of someone's messenger was tantamount to rejection of the sender himself. In many non-Western societies, honor and shame are of utmost importance. Dishonoring of a person is regarded as inexcusable.

Will never see death (8:51). The phrase is a common Jewish expression. It serves as "a graphic expression of the hard and painful reality of dying," stressing the bitter fate awaiting all human beings.[266] However, exceptions such as Enoch or Elijah showed that the power of death was not absolute.

Abraham died and so did the prophets (8:52). The Old Testament Scriptures, Jewish tradition, and Greco-Roman beliefs agree that death is the common lot of humanity. "What man can live and not see death, or save himself from the power of the grave?" writes the psalmist (Ps. 89:48). "Where are your forefathers now? And the prophets, do they live forever?" declares the prophet (Zech. 1:5). Even people the Jews believed to have been exceptionally close to God were not exempt from death. A later rabbinic passage narrates God's response to Moses when the latter expresses reluctance to die: "Behold Abraham, who honored my name in the world and died" (*Tanḥ.* 6:11). Greco-Roman culture concurs. The great classical Greek poet Homer queries, "Now, friend, do you too die? Why do you lament thus?" (*Iliad* 21.107). Lucretius, a first-century b.c. writer, echoes these sentiments: "And the Master ... Epicurus himself died.... And will *you* kick and protest against your sentence?" (*De Rer. Nat.* 3.1037–50).

You do not know him (8:55). The Jews do not "know" God, because they fail to "acknowledge" him. A similar charge was leveled against the Jews by some of the Old Testament prophets (e.g., Hos. 4:1; 6:6). Several later prophetic passages predict a time when people *would* know God (e.g., Isa. 11:9; Jer. 31:31–34; Hab. 2:14). But even the prophets could not claim to be free from sin or to know God the way Jesus claimed for himself.

Your father Abraham rejoiced at the thought of seeing my day; he saw it and was glad (8:56). "To say that Abraham saw the Messiah was neither new nor offensive to Jewish teachers; it was its application to Jesus that was unbelievable." Appealing to Genesis 15:17–21, R. Akiba (d. c. a.d. 135) taught that God revealed to Abraham the mysteries of the coming age (*Gen. Rab.* 44:22; *4 Ezra* 3:14; *2 Bar.* 4:4; *Apoc. Abr.* 31). Abraham's "rejoicing" was taken by Jewish tradition to refer to his laughter at the prospect (or actual birth) of his son Isaac. This interpretation was based partly on Genesis 17:17 (interpreted as joy, not scorn, as in Philo, *Names* 154–69) and partly on Genesis 21:6 (cf. *Jub.* 15:17; 16:19–29; see also *Tg. Onq.*). It has been suggested that the reference here may be to Abraham's rejoicing when he announced to Isaac on the way to the sacrifice, "God himself will provide the lamb for the burnt offering, my son" (Gen. 22:8). In *Testament of Levi* 18:2, 6, Levi predicts the coming of a "new priest" for whom "the heavens will be opened, and from the temple of glory sanctification will come upon him, with a fatherly voice, as from Abraham to Isaac."

My day (8:56). The "day of the Lord" here has become *Jesus'* "day." While this expression usually refers to the final judgment, here it probably denotes his incarnation.

You are not yet fifty years old (8:57). According to Luke 3:23, Jesus was about thirty years old when he began his ministry. If this is the fall of A.D. 32, Jesus would be about thirty-five (perhaps almost thirty-six) years old. The age of fifty was commonly considered to mark the end of a man's working life and his attainment of full maturity (cf. Num. 4:3, 39; 8:24–25; *m. 'Abot* 5:21: "at fifty for counsel"). Jesus, the Jews may be saying, has not even reached full maturity, and he makes claims such as having seen Abraham. Also, the book of *Jubilees* uses "fifty years" to measure the eras since the creation. Note also the interesting reference in *Pesiq. Rab.* 21:12: "The letter *nun*, whose numerical value is fifty, signifies that Abraham was fifty years old when he recognized his Maker."

Before Abraham was born, I am (8:58). Jesus' language here echoes God's self-identification to Moses in Exodus 3:14 (cf. Isa. 43:10, 13). Thus Jesus does not merely claim preexistence—or he could have said, "before Abraham was born, I *was*"—but deity (see the people's reaction in 8:59). Note also *Gospel of Thomas* 19: "Jesus said, 'Blessed is he who came into being before he came into being.' "

> **At this, they picked up stones to stone him (8:59).** Stoning was the prescribed punishment for blasphemy (Lev. 24:16; cf. Deut. 13:6–11; *m. Sanh.* 7:4). However, such punishment was to be the result of righteous judgment, not mob violence (Deut. 17:2–7). Already in Old Testament times, people considered stoning righteous men such as Moses (Ex. 17:4), Joshua and Caleb (Num. 14:10), or David (1 Sam. 30:6). Stephen, the church's first martyr, was stoned on account of alleged blasphemy (Acts 7:57–60). Paul, too, was stoned repeatedly, although he escaped with his life (Acts 14:19; 2 Cor. 11:25), as were other Christian saints (Heb. 11:37). The availability of stones in the temple area points to the fact that the temple was still being renovated (cf. John 2:20; Josephus, *Ant.* 17.9.3 §216; *J.W.* 2.1.3 §§11–12).[22]

Bible Background Craig S. Keener

8:57-58. Although the main point is that Jesus is too young to have known Abraham, his interlocutors might also imply that he is too young for much authority; fifty was the minimum age for involvement in some kinds of public service (and maximum for some others, Num 8:25). If Jesus merely wished to imply that he existed before Abraham, he should have said, "Before Abraham was, I was." But "I am" was a title for God (Ex 3:14), which suggests that Jesus is claiming more than that he merely existed before Abraham. This title of God may have been fresh on the minds of Jesus' hearers at the feast: later tradition says that during the Feast of Tabernacles, the priests uttered God's words in Isaiah: "I am the Lord, I am

---

[22] Clinton E. Arnold, *Zondervan Illustrated Bible Backgrounds Commentary: John, Acts.*, vol. 2 (Grand Rapids, MI: Zondervan, 2002), 85–91.

he" (Is 43:10, 13; the *Septuagint of Is 43:10 has ego eimi "I am"). (Although we cannot be certain of this tradition's date, it certainly does not derive from this Gospel.)[23]

Exegetical Commentary D. A. Carson

8:58. Once more Jesus solemnly announces, *I tell you the truth* (*cf.* notes on 1:51). If he had wanted to claim only that he existed before Abraham, it would have been simpler to say, 'Before Abraham was, I was'. Instead, bringing forward the use of *egō eimi* found in vv. 24, 28, Jesus says, 'Before Abraham was born, *I am*'. Whatever doubts may attach themselves to whether or not *egō eimi* should be taken absolutely in vv. 24, 28, here there can be none. Moreover, the strong linguistic connections with Isaiah 40–55 are supported by obvious conceptual links: *cf.* 'I, the Lord—with the first of them and with the last—*I am he*' (Is. 41:4); 'Yes, and from ancient days I am he' (Is. 43:13). *cf.* Ps. 90:2. That the Jews take up stones to kill him presupposes that they understand these words as some kind of blasphemous claim to deity. Nevertheless, as in 1:1, so here: neither the Word nor the Son is so identified with God that there is no remainder. *Cf.* notes on v. 24.

Abraham looked forward to the messianic age, the age that was, in John's understanding, inaugurated by the incarnation of the Word who already was 'in the beginning' (1:1), like God, eternal. In conformity with John's Prologue, Jesus takes to himself one of the most sacred of divine expressions of self-reference, and makes the *assumption* of that expression the proof of his superiority over Abraham (a point rather muddied by

---

[23] The IVP Bible Background Commentary: New Testament – Craig S. Keener, p. 275

66

Greek Grammar Daniel Wallace: The Force of the Historical Present

John 8:58

The text reads: πρὶν Ἀβραὰμ γενέσθαι ἐγὼ **εἰμί** ("before Abraham was, **I am**"). On this text, Dennis Light wrote an article in defense of the *New World Translation* in the *Bible Collector* (July-December, 1971). In his article he discusses ἐγὼ εἰμί, which the *New World Translation* renders, "I have been." Light defends this translation by saying, "The Greek verb *eimi*, literally present tense, must be viewed as a historical present, because of being preceded by the aorist infinitive clause referring to Abraham's past" (p. 8). This argument has several flaws in it: (1) The fact that the present tense follows an aorist *infinitive* has nothing to do with how it should be rendered. In fact, historical presents are usually wedged in between aorist (or imperfect) *indicatives*, not infinitives. (2) If this is a historical present, it is apparently the only historical present in the NT that uses the equative verb εἰμί. The burden of proof, therefore, lies with one who sees εἰμί as *ever* being used as a historical present. (3) If this is a historical present, it is apparently the only historical present in the NT that is in other than the third person.[25]

---

24 D. A. Carson, *The Gospel according to John*, The Pillar New Testament Commentary (Leicester, England; Grand Rapids, MI: Inter-Varsity Press; W.B. Eerdmans, 1991), 358.

25 47. To be sure, εἰμί is sometimes considered to be a historical present as is the first person verb, but most reject these identifications in the passages suggested. (Cf. the treatments of this issue in R. L. Shive, "The Historical Present in the New Testament," and D. B. Wallace, "John

The translators of the *New World Translation* understand the implications of ἐγὼ εἰμί here, for in the footnote to this text in the *NWT*, they reveal their motive for seeing this as a historical present: "It is not the same as ὁ ὤν (*ho ohn´*, meaning 'The Being'

531

or 'The I Am') at Exodus 3:14, *LXX*." In effect, this is a negative admission that if ἐγὼ εἰμί is *not* a historical present, then Jesus is here claiming to be the one who spoke to Moses at the burning bush, the I AM, the eternally existing One, Yahweh (cf. Exod 3:14 in the LXX, ἐγὼ εἰμι ὁ ὤν).[26]

Textual Scholar Brooke Foss Westcott

> **58.** There can be no doubt as to the meaning of the final answer which follows as a natural climax to

5, 2 and the Date of the Fourth Gospel," *Bib* 71 [1990] 177-205.) A proper syntactical approach must be based on legitimate, undisputed examples. Disputed examples must fit into the contours of such clear instances or be judged suspect. This is not to say that it is *impossible* for εἰμί to be a historical present in, say, John 8:58. But it is to say that the burden of proof rests with the one who makes such a claim. Unfortunately, a typical approach to grammar in such disputed passages is (a) to locate a category of usage that fits one's preconceived views, and (b) to ignore the semantic situation of the category and to argue on the basis of context (which must be construed) and ingenuity. Context, of course, has its rather large place in exegesis—larger for the most part than grammar—but our contention is that grammar is often relegated to a mere pool of options.

[26] 48. More nuanced is the view that εἰμί is a present tense extending from the past (so McKay, *New Syntax*, 42). However, John 8:58 lacks sufficient parallels to be convincing.

Daniel B. Wallace, *Greek Grammar Beyond the Basics - Exegetical Syntax of the New Testament* (Zondervan Publishing House and Galaxie Software, 1996), 530–531.

what had been said before. Abraham died: Christ was the Giver of life. Abraham was the father of the Jews: Christ was the centre of Abraham's hope. Abraham came into being as a man: Christ is essentially as God. And this closing revelation is prefaced by the solemn words which fix attention upon its substance. *Verily, verily, I say unto you, Before Abraham was*—was born, came to be—*I am* (πρὶν Ἀ. γενέσθαι ἐγώ εἰμι, Vulg. *antequam fieret Abraham ego sum*).

I am] The phrase marks a timeless existence. In this connexion "I was" would have expressed simple priority. Thus there is in the phrase the contrast between the created and the uncreated, and the temporal and the eternal. At the same time the ground of the assurance in *v.* 51 is made known. The believer lives because Christ lives, and lives with an absolute life (comp. 14:19).[27]

Senior Bible Translator NASB Don Wilkins

John 8:58

Let's look now at John 8:58, a verse for which the translation is not so easily evaluated. Here is a word-for-word translation:

Jesus said to them, "Truly, truly I say to you, before Abraham came to be, I am."

The word "truly" is an approximation for "amen" in the Greek, which is a transliteration of the Hebrew. Since we have a fairly good working understanding of the word,

---

[27] Brooke Foss Westcott and Arthur Westcott, eds., *The Gospel according to St. John Introduction and Notes on the Authorized Version*, Classic Commentaries on the Greek New Testament (London: J. Murray, 1908), 140.

it might be just as well to translate, "Amen, amen I say to you...." The word "came to be" can be understood as Abraham's birth, and has been translated by some as "was," i.e. simple existence.

The challenging part, however, is the clause "I am." It is a grammatical mismatch with the dependent adverbial clause "before Abraham came to be," both in English and in Greek. That is, the timing is off: "I am" is present tense, but it should have been past tense to have been happening before Abraham's time. Not surprisingly, therefore, one significant ancient manuscript omits "came to be," which would provide a little wiggle room out of the problem. But this just serves to confirm the reading "I am," and we are left to conclude either that Jesus actually said this, or that John made a mistake in his reporting. A slip of the pen would not account for it, and we have nothing elsewhere in John's writings similar to it, so translators and other scholars are agreed that Jesus said it.

Speaking again as a translator for the NASB, I can tell you that it is NASB policy to do translation that is grammatically correct English; but this constitutes an exception. Furthermore, there is an unwritten rule of creativity for experts of any language: when you know the rules, you are entitled to break the rules occasionally for special effect. Jesus certainly would have been aware of the grammatical mismatch that he had articulated, and John knew better than to correct it.

The best thing that the translator of a literal Bible can do with this grammatical anomaly is to retain the literal present tense of the verb "I am"; indeed, it is probably wise even for DE/FE translators to do this, and this is what we usually see. But many translators have not been content with this, given the awkward grammar. They have sought the reason for Jesus' choice of wording, and most believe that they have found it in Ex. 3:14, where God gives Moses "I Am" as the name that he is to pass on to his fellow Israelites when they ask for God's name.

This discovery has in turn led to a biased handling of the clause in some translations (keeping in mind that "bias" is not necessarily bad). Sometimes it is seen in the text. The NASB has "I AM" in Ex. 3:14 in all capital letters both for emphasis and to reflect the fact that the clause was used as a proper name. This is typical for all translations, not just the NASB. However, in earlier editions, the NASB also had "I AM" in John 8:58 in all capital letters to indicate that Jesus had used God's words in Ex. 3:14 as his own. The NLT does this, and probably a few other versions. Virtually all translations, with the notable exception of the NWT, cross reference Ex. 3:14 to Jesus' statement and some make the connection explicit with a note (cp. the HCSB).

I think it is accurate to say that this is not a case where translators are forced to choose between one theological position and another. The connection to Ex. 3:14, if credible, just provides an explanation for the grammatical mismatch. We can attempt to make sense of Jesus' statement without resorting to Ex. 3:14, by saying for example that he wanted to stump his opponents by using an odd construction. In the end, all the translator really has to do in this case is to provide a translation consistent with his translation philosophy, and if he chooses, he can provide Ex. 3:14 as a cross-reference. This is what the NASB translators decided to do for the updated edition.

Linking John 8:58 to Ex. 3:14 of course has the effect of turning Jesus' words into a proof text for his deity, so the question of whether the connection is credible carries extra weight. As one would expect, the NWT translators have strongly objected to the connection, and have argued that the claim that Jesus used the Greek of the LXX translation of Ex. 3:14 is false, since the latter has "he who exists" (or more literally "the one existing") instead of "I am." They are absolutely correct about the LXX, which was the standard Greek translation of the Hebrew Bible (i.e. the Old Testament) in the first century.

However, like the argument about "a" for John 1:1, this argument about the wording of the LXX proves to be irrelevant.[28] The LXX translators were trying to put the actual Hebrew of Ex. 3:14 into better, less literal Greek. Jesus, on the other hand, clearly chose either the literal Hebrew or a literal Greek translation of the Hebrew. Which of these he did is–to me at least–a fascinating question, deserving of a dissertation for which (fortunately for the reader) there is insufficient space here. Just to give the faintest outline of what I mean, when Jesus said "I am," he was speaking Aramaic, or Greek, or using the Hebrew of Ex. 3:14. John, in turn, was either translating Jesus' words or copying them when he eventually recorded them in his gospel. In any case, I take great comfort in my personal conviction that the Bible is inspired and completely inerrant, so I can fully trust that what John wrote was what Jesus meant.

Now it so happens that Hebrew does not have a direct grammatical equivalent of the Greek "I am" that John wrote down. The Hebrew of Ex. 3:14 is rather flexible, in fact, as one can see by looking at commentaries and comparing marginal notes on it. Ordinarily, the form that we find in Ex. 3:14 would be translated as the future ("I will be"), or occasionally as the past–technically the imperfect tense–depending on the context. So how is it that we find "I am" in Ex. 3:14? It is a matter of contextual interpretation, which we discussed in chapter 2. While present time is not the usual meaning of the Hebrew construction, it is a possible meaning, and neither the past

---

[28] It also strikes me as being a kind of "straw man" argument in that I do not think a knowledgeable orthodox apologist would make it; it would only benefit the opposing side.

("I was") nor the future ("I will be") would make good sense in this context.[29]

So then, let's assume the level of bias in John 8:58 that would be represented by "I AM" in all capital letters. How should we evaluate it? If the connection to Ex. 3:14 can be justified, it becomes a proof text for the deity of Christ, and thus it is good bias from the orthodox viewpoint, or very bad bias from the opposing viewpoint.

Is the connection credible? The two constructions have grammatical awkwardness in common: "I AM has sent me" and "Before Abraham was born I AM." Also, *if* Jesus had the "I AM" of Ex. 3:14 in mind, he makes the connection stronger, not weaker, by using the literal Greek for "I am" instead of the LXX's more polished "the one who exists."

On the other hand, the contexts are entirely different. In Ex. 3:14 "I AM" is simply the answer to a question, a verb used as a proper noun, to be accepted as the equivalent of the name of God. In John 8:58 "I am" is a verbal statement used in the normal way, except for the mismatch in timing. It is intended to correct the mistaken conclusion of Jesus' opponents. If Jesus had used a simple past tense, saying, "Before Abraham was born, I existed," would we make the same connection to Ex. 3:14? I am almost certain that we would not. Ironically, however, the verb form in the Greek would be a grammatical match to the Hebrew "I AM" of Ex. 3:14; so again, it is the awkwardness that seems to connect them. And if we could assume the fact of the connection, then Jesus' use of the present tense would testify to "I AM" as the correct

---

[29] This has not stopped some translators who for one reason or another are fixated on elementary Hebrew grammar from choosing a form of the future. The more experienced translators who choose to acknowledge the common use of the future tense confine the option to a marginal note.

translation in Ex. 3:14; but that would be begging the question.

Another thing to consider in evaluating the bias is the possibility of collateral benefits or damage to orthodox theology. The same issue comes into view here that we saw in John 1:1, i.e. the possibility of confusing the Father with the Son. In 1:1, fortunately, the use of the article distinguished the two. Here, however, if the connection is valid, we have the voice from the burning bush and Jesus saying the same thing about themselves. The voice is that of the God of Israel, or more specifically from a Trinitarian viewpoint, that of the Father. Can Jesus say "I AM" without making himself the Father? Or is this a proof text that might prove to do as much harm to orthodox theology as it does good?

This is another dissertation-level issue that I will refrain from elaborating here. There are certain theological phenomena in the Bible that seem to allow overlap in the persons of the Father and the Son without actually confusing them. The "Angel of Jehovah[30]" is one, thought by many to be the pre-incarnate Christ speaking in the first person as the direct representative of the Father. There is also the possibility that whenever God appeared to man in the Old Testament, it was actually the pre-incarnate Christ. Also, in the description of the coming Messiah in Is. 9:6, we have among his several titles not only "Mighty God" but the surprising "Eternal Father." And of course we also have Christ telling Philip, "He who has seen me has seen the Father; how can you say, 'Show us the Father'?" (John 14:9). So closely and intimately does Jesus represent the Father that we can expect to see him speaking as the

---

[30] It is translated "angel of the LORD" in the NASB and a number of other versions; I used the more traditional wording.

Father. Yet he also clearly distinguishes himself from the Father.

Therefore, while I like the connection to Ex. 3:14 and its implication of deity for Jesus, and I do not think that it necessarily poses the problem of confusing the Father with the Son, I also think that there is laudable wisdom in handling "I am" in John 8:58 with restraint. A moderate approach is to put the words in plain text, while including a cross reference to Ex. 3:14, as the NASB translators did in the updated edition, and has been done in a number of other translations.

CHAPTER 2 The Second View on Translating John 8:58

First, it should be stated that every Christian has some theological bias to them, even Bible scholars, which would include Bible translators and textual scholars. Yet, bias affects some more than others. Thus, for the translator, it is simply a matter of how much are you going to allow your biases to impact you. Then, there are publishers who actually control the Bible translation, and, in many cases, their bottom line is sales, not accuracy. They may feel that a verse that supports a particular doctrinal position, which all one hundred translators know for a fact was not in the original but was added by a copyist centuries later is too important to the Christians who buy their Bible so they will retain that verse that all know to be an interpolation so that there is no detrimental impact on the sales. **Second**, because one is theologically biased over a verse, this does not mean that what he says about it is wrong. Does he ignore the best textual evidence to retain a preferred verse? Does he violate grammar rules that he applies correctly elsewhere to retain a preferred rendering? This is evidence that theological bias has impacted him.

John 8:58 is one of the most hotly debated verses in the Bible, so our investigation begins and ends here.

UASV	ESV, LEB, HCSB, RSV	NLV	CEV
Jesus said to them, "Most truly I say to you, *Before*	Jesus said to them, "Truly, truly, I say to you,	Jesus said to them, "For sure, I tell you, before	Jesus answered, "I tell you for certain that even

Abraham was, I am." [*]	*before* Abraham was, I am."	Abraham was born, I was and am and always will be!"	before Abraham was, I was, and I am."
NLT	NAB	TEV, GNT	NASB, ASV
Jesus answered, "I tell you the truth, *before* Abraham was even born, I Am!	Jesus said to them, "Amen, amen, I say to you, *before* Abraham came to be, I AM."	"I am telling you the truth," Jesus replied. "*Before* Abraham was born, 'I AM'."	Jesus said to them, "Truly, truly, I say to you, before Abraham was born, I am."

John 8:58 American Translation (AT) Jesus said to them, "I tell you, I existed *before* Abraham was born!"

[*] The literal rendering is (Greek, ego' eimi') "I am." However, the Greek to English grammatically correct rendering should be "… before Abraham came to be I have been in existence." K. L. McKay, A New Syntax of the Verb in New Testament Greek (New York: Peter Lang, 1994), p. 42. Having [before Abraham / came to be / I am] as far as English word order is fine, but we are violating verb compatibility, mixing a present tense with a past tense, which is not grammatically correct. In both Greek and English, we would put or find our past tense first, followed by the present tense; logically reasoning that the past happened before the present. However, the adverb "before" affects this decision, for it informs us that the action expressed by our present tense verb ("am") not

only began in the past, but it was before our past tense verb ("came to be"), and up unto our past tense verb and still in progress at the time this clause was uttered. The other translations have been following the grammar rule known as PPA, the Present of Past Action still in progress in several other places in John's Gospel (14:9; 15:27, etc.), wherein a present indicative ("I am" or "you are"), which is accompanied by an adverbial expression ("so much time" or "from the beginning" or "before"), is rendered with the perfect tense of "have been." The PPA is describing an action that began in the past and has run up unto the time of writing or speaking.

The most important interpretation rule is the context. The question is, do we find the context of John 8:58 as being in harmony with our grammar. Well, let us look at the verse(s) that come before and after our verse. In verse 57, the Jews ask a question in reference to Jesus' statement in verse 56: "Your father Abraham rejoiced that he would see my day. He saw it and was glad." Thus, they reasonably ask, "You are not yet fifty years old and have you seen Abraham?" It is all too clear that we have a question that is based on age, not Jesus' identity. Our historical-cultural question is addressed in verse 59, where we find the Jews seeking to stone Jesus for his response. What was there about Jesus' response that would result in their attempt to stone him? First, to claim to have been in existence since before Abraham and up unto this point; would mean Jesus was/is a divine person. Bible scholar Kenneth L. McKay wrote: "to claim to have been in existence for so long is in itself a staggering one, quite enough to provoke the crowd's violent reaction." – McKay: *The Expository Times*, 1996, p. 302.

How We Got There

Throughout this entire publication, we have preached the importance of the literal translation philosophy. However, we have repeatedly said that there are two exceptions to the literal, philosophical position, **(1)** if the rendering ends up nonsensical, or **(2)** the rendering presents misinformation. As you can see from the above, there are several different things going on:

(1) Some are trying to remain to what they believe is literal (RSV, ESV, LEB, and UASV),

(2) Others are trying to get at the sense of what Jesus meant by the words that he used and how he used them (ASV, UASV (ftn.), and NASB).

(3) Some are demonstrating theological bias (NLT, NAB, TEV and GNT).

Before we begin our investigation, first, let us consider some sound advice from the chief translator of the Good News Bible (TEV) Robert Bratcher:

"At least it can be agreed that any translation, in order to be considered good, should satisfy three requirements: **(1)** it should handle textual matters in an informed and responsible way. . . . **(2)** Its exegesis of the original texts should be theologically unbiased ... **(3)** Its language should be contemporary; it should conform to normal English usage. – Bratcher 1978, pp 115-116.

First, we do not have to worry about any textual problem with John 8:58. However, his very translation, the Today's English Version (TEV) violated point number 2, in that his team's exegesis was certainly theologically biased here at John 8:58. As to point number 3, we have already stated our position on that through this publication. Now, before we delve into how the NLT, NAB, TEV, and GNT are theologically biased here, let us look at the original Greek.

KATA ΙΩANNHN 8:58 The Greek-English New Testament Interlinear (GENTI)

<table>
<tr><td>Said</td><td>to them</td><td>Jesus</td><td>Truly</td><td>truly</td><td>I</td><td>say</td><td>to you</td><td>Before</td><td>Abraham</td><td>to</td><td>become</td><td>I</td><td>am</td></tr>
<tr><td colspan="14">58 εἶπεν αὐτοῖς Ἰησοῦς Ἀμὴν ἀμὴν λέγω ὑμῖν, πρὶν Ἀβραάμ γενέσθαι ἐγὼ εἰμί.</td></tr>
</table>

An interlinear study tool is not interested in grammar and syntax (how words are joined together to make sense), but rather only in the lexical English corresponding equivalent. Therefore, the first person, personal pronoun *ego* would be rendered "I" and the present, active, indicative, verb *eimi* would be rendered "am." It is not until we bring our lexical glosses over into English that we begin our investigation of the grammar and syntax.

John 8:58 Grammar and Syntax

Before
- **πρὶν** Adjective Adverb ["before"] (adverbial past time expression)

Abraham
- Αβραὰμ Noun Accusative ["Abraham"] (Direct Object)

to become
- γενέσθαι Verb Infinitive Aorist Middle-Deponent ["came to be"] (past tense)

I
- ἐγὼ Noun Pronoun Nominal ["I"] (Subject)

am.
- εἰμί. Verb Indicative Present Active ("I am")

Having [before Abraham / came to be / I am] as far as English word order is fine, but we are violating verb compatibility, mixing a present tense with a past tense, which is not grammatically correct. In both Greek and English, we would put or find our past tense first, followed by the present tense; logically reasoning that the past happened before the present. However, the adverb "before" affects this decision, for it informs us that the action expressed by our present tense verb ("am") not only began in the past, but it was before our past tense verb ("came to be"), and up unto our past tense verb and still in progress at the time this clause was uttered.

Lexical-Syntactical Analysis and Comparison

In this stage, we will continue with our look at individual words (lexicology), but we will also take a deeper look into our new stage of how these words are dealt with in concert with each other (syntax). However, to avoid theological bias, we will look at two other examples of this same grammatical construction in the Gospel of John first, staying outside of the highly theologically charged John 8:58 at this time, to see how other translations deal with the grammatical construction before rendering John 8:58.

John 14:9 The Greek-English New Testament Interlinear (GENTI)

9 λέγει αὐτῷ ὁ Ἰησοῦς Τοσοῦτον χρόνον μεθ᾽ ὑμῶν εἰμι καὶ οὐκ ἔγνωκάς με.

Literal: <u>So much</u> time with you <u>I am</u>

The "I am" present indicative of John 14:9 is 'modified' by the past time expression "so much time." How do our translations render this verse? Do they ignore the grammar rules, using present tense ("I am"), or do they follow the grammar rules that we are about to discuss, and use a perfect tense ("have been")? Our translations below do follow the grammar rule.

ESV	NASB	ASV	HCSB
<u>Have I been</u> with you so long	<u>Have I been</u> so long with you	<u>Have I been</u> so long time with you	<u>Have I been</u> among you all this time

The "you are" present indicative of **John 15:27** is 'modified' by the past time expression "from the beginning."

ESV	NASB	ASV	HCSB
you <u>have been</u> with me from the beginning	you <u>have been</u> with Me from the beginning	ye <u>have been</u> with me from the beginning	you <u>have been</u> with Me from the beginning

Greek Grammar

At this point, it is time to visit the Greek grammars, looking for this particular construction that we have found in John 8:58, as well as all throughout the Gospel of John. The grammar rule for a present tense that is found positioned with an adverbial expression of past time and duration is largely known as a PPA

Moulton's references Ernest De Witt Burton in his *Syntax of the Moods and Tenses in N.T. Greek*, 'The Tenses,' par.17, p.10, we can read: "17. **The Present of Past Action still in progress [PPA]**. The Present Indicative, accompanied by an adverbial expression denoting duration and referring to past time, is sometimes used in Greek, as in German, to describe an action which, beginning in past time, is still in progress at the time of speaking. English idiom requires the use of the Perfect in such cases." Bold and underline is mine.

A Manual Grammar of the Greek New Testament, by Dana and Mantey, MacMillan, 1927, p. 183, says, "Sometimes the progressive present is retroactive in its application, denoting that which has begun in the past and continued into the present. For the want of a better name, we may call it the present of duration. This use is generally associated with an adverb of time and may best be rendered by the English perfect. "Ye have been (present tense) with me from the beginning" John 15:27."

A Grammar of New Testament Greek, by J. H. Moulton, Vol. III, by Nigel Turner, Edinburgh, 1963, p. 62, says, "The Present which indicates the continuance of an action during the past and up to the moment of speaking is virtually the same as Perfective, the only difference being that the action is conceived as still in progress . . . It is frequent in the N[ew] T[estament]· Lk 2^{48} 13^7 , , , 15^{29} . . . Jn 5^6 8^{58} . . . "

Greek Grammar for Colleges, by Herbert Weir Smyth, New York, 1920, pp. 422-423: "The present, when accompanied by a definite or indefinite expression of past time, is used to express an action begun in the past and continued in the present. The 'progressive perfect' is often used in translation. Thus, ... **I have been long** (and am still) **wondering**."

The Expository Times, 1996, page 302 by Kenneth McKay says, "The verb 'to be' is used differently, in what is presumably its basic meaning of 'be in existence', in John 8:58: *prin Abraam genesthai ego eimi*, which would be most naturally translated 'I have been in existence since before Abraham was born', if it were not for the obsession with the simple words 'I am'. If we take the Greek words in their natural meaning, as we surely should, the claim to have been in existence for so long is in itself a staggering one, quite enough to provoke the crowd's violent reaction."

As we can see, the translations have been following the grammar rule known as PPA, the Present of Past Action still in progress, where in a present indicative ("I am" or "you are"), which is accompanied by an adverbial expression ("so much time" or "from the beginning"), is rendered with the perfect tense of "have been." The PPA is describing an action that began in the past and has run up unto the time of writing or speaking. Let us pause and look at two more examples.

John 8:24 The Greek-English New Testament Interlinear (GENTI)

24 εἶπον οὖν ὑμῖν ὅτι ἀποθανεῖσθε ἐν ταῖς ἁμαρτίαις ὑμῶν· ἐὰν γὰρ μὴ πιστεύσητε ὅτι ἐγώ εἰμι, ἀποθανεῖσθε ἐν ταῖς ἁμαρτίαις ὑμῶν.

We have an implied predicate nominative ("he") that comes after the "I am."

ESV	NASB	ASV	HCSB
for unless you believe that I am **he** you will die in your sins.	for unless you believe that I am **He**, you will die in your sins.	for except ye believe that I am **he**, ye shall die in your sins.	for unless you believe that I am **He**, you will die in your sins."

Notice that all of these translations recognize the implied predicate nominative ("he") that comes after the "I am."

John 4:26 The Greek-English New Testament Interlinear (GENTI)

26 λέγει αὐτῇ ὁ Ἰησοῦς Ἐγώ εἰμι, ὁ λαλῶν σοι.

Here in John chapter 4, you have Jesus being spoken to by a Samaritan woman. She is inquiring about the coming Messiah, and Jesus does something with the Samaritan woman that he has not done even with his disciples, He discloses who he really is, "I am the one" [i.e., the Messiah]. The ESV, like the other translations that we have considered, is aware that there is an implied predicate pronoun in the sentence "I am [he] the one speaking to you."

ESV	NASB	ASV	HCSB
Jesus said to her, "I who speak to you am he."	Jesus said to her, "I who speak to you am He."	Jesus saith unto her, I that speak unto thee am he.	"I am **He**," Jesus told her, "the One speaking to you."

The predicate nominative is supplied from context in the English translation.

John 13:19 The Greek-English New Testament Interlinear (GENTI)

19 ἀπ' ἄρτι λέγω ὑμῖν πρὸ τοῦ γενέσθαι, ἵνα πιστεύητε ὅταν γένηται ὅτι ἐγώ εἰμι.

The Lexham English Bible writes in a footnote, "Here the predicate nominative ("*he*") is understood but must be supplied in the translation." Again, our other translations recognize this.

ESV	NASB	ASV	HCSB
I am telling you this now, before it takes place, that when it does take place you may believe that I am he.	From now on I am telling you before it comes to pass, so that when it does occur, you may believe that I am He.	From henceforth I tell you before it come to pass, that, when it is come to pass, ye may believe that I am **he.**	I am telling you now before it happens, so that when it does happen you will believe that I am **He.**

Jesus is merely pointing to himself as a fulfillment of the prophecy in which one of his closest disciples would betray him. (See John 13:18 and Psalm 41:9)

Context, Context, Context

The most important interpretation rule is the context. All along, our grammar has been telling us about the PPA rule. The PPA is describing an action that began in the past and had run up unto the time of writing or speaking. The question is, do we find the context of John 8:58 as being in harmony with our grammar. Well, let us look at the verse(s) that come before and after our verse. In verse 57, the Jews ask a question in reference to Jesus statement in verse 56: "Your father Abraham rejoiced that he would see my day. He saw it and was glad." Thus, they reasonably ask, "You are not yet fifty years old and have you seen Abraham?" It is all too clear that we have a question that is based on age, not Jesus' identity.

86

John 8:56-59 New American Standard Bible (NASB)	John 8:56-59 Updated American Standard Version (UASV)
56 Your father Abraham rejoiced to see My day, and he saw *it* and was glad." 57 So the Jews said to Him, "You are not yet fifty years old, and have You seen Abraham?" 58 Jesus said to them, "Truly, truly, I say to you, before Abraham was born, I am." 59 Therefore they picked up stones to throw at Him, but Jesus hid Himself and went out of the temple.	56 Your father Abraham rejoiced that he would see my day. He saw it and rejoiced." 57 So the Jews said to him, "You are not yet fifty years old, and have you seen Abraham?" 58 Jesus said to them, "Truly, truly, I say to you, before Abraham was I am." 59 So they picked up stones to throw at him, but Jesus hid himself and went out of the temple.

From the context, John 8:58 would seem to have no meaning in the way of expressing existence or some kind of identity. Why are we even saying this? Because the translators have long maintained that that the "I am" is not predicated. In other words, for them the "I am" is absolute, a reference to what they perceive to be the divine name in Exodus 3:14.[31] These translators believe that the "I AM" as they render it is a title for Jesus, which ties him into Exodus 3:14, which is rendered, "God replied to Moses, 'I AM who I AM. Say this to the people of Israel: I AM has sent me to you.'" Notice that the NLT capitalizes the "I AM" in both John 8:58 and Exodus 3:14. There is no objective reason to capitalize the "I AM." It is

---

[31] **Exodus 3:14 New Living Translation (NLT)** 14 God replied to Moses, "I AM who I AM. Say this to the people of Israel: I AM has sent me to you."

completely subjective, in that their agenda is to tie Jesus in with Exodus 3:14. However, that alone is a problem, because Exodus 3:14 is referring to the Father, and John 8:58 is referring to the Son, Jesus, his length of existence actually. Therefore, the Son and the Father are two separate persons. Moreover, the context is not about the person of Jesus or his title, but the length of his existence, i.e., how long he has been around. In addition, how should Exodus 3:14 be rendered?

Exodus 3:14 Updated American Standard Version (UASV)

14 God said to Moses, "I will be what I will be" And he said, "Say this to the people of Israel: 'I will be sent me to you.'"

In Exodus 3:13, Moses had just asked God a very important question. "Behold, I am going to the sons of Israel, and I will say to them, 'The God of your fathers has sent me to you.' Now they may say to me, 'What is his name?' What shall I say to them?" God, then replied,

to   be   to   become,   prove   to   be   who   to   be   to   become   prove   to   be
אֱהְיר Eh·yeh' (הָיָה ha·yah')- אֲשֶׁר ('Asher') אֶהְיֶה Eh·yeh' (הָיָה ha·yah').

This has nothing to do with whether God existed or not but rather what that Father intended "to become" toward his people and by extension all of his servants. Therefore, the Updated American Standard Version correctly renders the above Hebrew expression as "I will be what I will be." God the Father then added: "Say this to the people of Israel: 'I will be sent me to you.'" (Ex 3:14) God was in no way making some change to his divine name, but rather he was giving Moses, Aaron, and the enslaved Israelites insight into His personality, which is evidenced by what he said next: "Thus you shall say to the sons of Israel, 'Jehovah, the God of your fathers, the God of Abraham, the God of Isaac, and the God of Jacob, has sent me to you.' This is my name forever, and this is how I am to be remembered from generation to generation." (Ex 3:15) The divine name Jehovah comes from the Hebrew verb (הָיָה ha·yah') "to be," or rather "to become," "to come to pass;" and therefore meaning, "He causes to become," "He brings to pass;" "The Fulfiller."[32] This definition certainly applies to Jehovah God, who was the Creator of everything and "The Fulfiller" of His will and purposes.

The New International Standard Bible Encyclopedia says:

"I will be who/what I will be...is preferable because the verb hayah [to be] has a more dynamic sense of being — not pure existence, but becoming, happening, being present — and because the historical and theological context of these early chapters of Exodus shows that God is revealing to Moses, and subsequently to the whole people, not the inner nature of His being [or existence], but his active, redemptive intentions on their behalf. He 'will be' to them 'what His deeds will show Him 'to be.'[33] "In Exodus 3:14 Jehovah is explained as equivalent to 'ehyeh, which is a short form of 'ehyeh 'asher 'ehyeh, translated in the RV [Revised Version] 'I am that I am.' ... the imperfect 'eheye is more accurately translated 'I will be what I will be,' a Semitic idiom meaning, 'I will be all that is necessary as the occasion will arise ' a familiar OT idea. (cf Is 7:4,9; Ps 23)."[34]

---

[32] Joseph S. Exell and Thomas H. Leale, *Genesis*, The Preacher's Complete Homiletic Commentary (New York; London; Toronto: Funk & Wagnalls Company, 1892), 39.

[33] Wright, C. J. H. (1982). Names of God. In Geoffrey W. Bromiley, Everett F. Harrison, Roland K. Harrison et. al. (Eds.), The International Standard Bible Encyclopedia, Volume Two. p. 507

[34] Ibid. p. 1254

Robert M. Bowman Jr. is an Evangelical Christian theologian specializing in the study of apologetics, who acknowledge, "It is true that the expression in Exodus 3:14 is probably better translated 'I will be what I will be' ..."[35] Bowman argued in another work of his, "most Hebraists now recognize [EHYEH] to mean literally, 'I will be,' with the connotation of 'I shall prove to be.' Although many evangelical scholars have argued that 'I am" is correct, there would appear to be solid reasons for accepting the rendering 'I will be' or 'I will become.' This would make the meaning of EHYEH ASHER EHYEH to be 'I will be what I will be,' or some such equivalent."[36] (bracketed words are mine)

The English Standard Version (ESV) renders Exodus 3:14 "God said to Moses, 'I AM WHO I AM.'" This is really going beyond the text. But we can say that at least the ESV footnote informs its readers that "I will be what I will be" is an acceptable alternative reading. The Anchor Bible notes, "If one could say 'I am that I am' in Hebrew at all, it would probably be through some such barbarous circumlocution as 'anoki hu' 'aser 'anoki hu'. Likewise, if the meaning were 'I am 'ehye(h),' as the second half of the verse might suggest, we would expect 'anoki (hu') 'ehye(h). An if the intention were ''ehye(h) is who I am' ... again assuming this could be conveyed in Hebrew at all, we should get something like 'ehye(h) 'aser 'anoki hu'. We still have the option of rendering 'ehye(h) 'aser 'ehye(h) as 'ehye(h) is who I will be,' but this seems a strange way for the Deity to identify himself. I follow, therefore, the translation of Aquila and Theodotion: esomai (hos) esomai 'I will be who I will be' ... Or, if the intent is

---

[35] Robert Bowman, Why You Should Believe in the Trinity, (Grand Rapids, MI, Baker Pub Group) 99.

[36] Robert M. Bowman Jr., The Jehovah's Witnesses, Jesus Christ, and the Gospel of John (Grand Rapids, MI, Baker Pub Group) 125.

evasion, an attractive alternative is 'I may be who I may be' ..., Notice how gradually Yahweh approaches the explicit pronouncement of his name: 'I will be who I will be. ('ehye[h] 'aser 'ehye[h]) ... 'I-will-be' ('ehye[h]) has sent me to you. ... Only the last truly answers Moses' question."[37]

Bible Background

Our historical-cultural question is addressed in verse 59, where we find the Jews seeking to stone Jesus for his response. What was there about Jesus' response that would result in their attempting to stone him? First, to claim to have been in existence since before Abraham and up unto this point; would mean Jesus was/is a divine person. Bible scholar Kenneth L. McKay wrote: "to claim to have been in existence for so long is in itself a staggering one, quite enough to provoke the crowd's violent reaction." – McKay: *The Expository Times*, 1996, p. 302.

Our "am" present indicative is 'modified' by the adverbial past time expression of *prin* (before), an adverb. In other words, **"Before** Abraham came to be." As many grammarians have suggested, getting the exact sense of the original Greek, it is best to render the present indicative "am" as the perfect indicative "have been." It is not only best, but also required as was said; the present indicative "am" is 'modified' to the perfect indicative "have been."

As was said earlier, a translation should reflect the meaning of the original Greek in English by way of being unbiased, accurate, clear, and natural. Is a translation *unbiased* to follow a grammatical construction in other parts of John when there is no theological significance at

---

[37] The Anchor Bible, Exodus 1-18, A New Translation with Introduction and Commentary (New York: Doubleday, 1999) 204-5.

stake, but to abandon this grammar at John 8:58? Is it *unbiased* to capitalize **εἰμί** (*eimi*) as "I AM" when there is absolutely no authority for such a decision? Is a translator *accurately* communicating the correct sense when he ignores the grammar and the context and takes it upon himself to render a verse based on his preconceived understanding? Is it *clear* if the reader is blocked by the translator's choice and is unable to achieve the correct mental understanding of the original writer? Does the translation that reads, "Before Abraham came to be, I AM," sound *natural* in our English language and is it appropriate?

Final Analysis

The final analysis is to ask how John 8:58b should be translated into English? Let us look for the bounds that we have set forth here in this chapter: grammatical, coherent and conveying what was meant, as well as the avoidance of intentional theological bias. Our objective is to follow the principle mentioned in Dr. Robert H. Stein's lectures, i.e., 'render it as it should be, if it supports a doctrinal position, so be it. However, if it does not support a doctrinal position, so be it as well. God does not need our help in conveying a doctrine. No doctrine is built on any one Scripture.'

John 8:58

Jesus said to them, "Amen, amen, I say to you, *before* **Abraham came to be, <u>I AM</u>**."

This is the most common rendering minus the capitalization of the "I AM." However, it falls short in many areas. First, it is not grammatically correct, because the English present come before some past time. This makes it incoherent, meaning that it does not convey the sense that Jesus was attempting to express. It has elements of theological bias because of the capitalization of the "I AM."

John 8:58

Jesus said to them, "Truly, truly, I say to you, *before* **Abraham came to be,** <u>I am</u>."

Again, this rendering falls short in at least two areas. First, it is not grammatically correct, because the English present come before some past time. This makes it incoherent, meaning that it does not convey these sense that Jesus was attempting to express.

John 8:58

Jesus said to them, "Truly, truly, I say to you, *before* **Abraham came into being,** <u>I was</u>."

This rendering is grammatically correct, making it coherent, and possesses some semblance of what Jesus meant. However, Jesus entire thought was that he was in existence prior to Abraham and had been living up unto his present conversation.

John 8:58

Jesus said to them, "Most truly I say to you, *Before* **Abraham came to be,** <u>I have been *in existence*</u>."

This is the least favored by most translators, even though they use "have been" with the same grammatical construction elsewhere in the Gospel of John. An earlier edition of the New American Standard Bible had "I have been" as a marginal note. It is not grammatical as far as English goes because a perfect cannot appear with specifying adverbials. However, it is coherent in that the reader now fully understand what Jesus meant about his being in existence prior to Abraham's being born and has existed up unto his current conversation. It is also the recommended rendering by the grammarians because of the present indicative "I am," which is accompanied by an adverbial expression "before," so it should be rendered with the perfect tense of "have been."

Translation that set aside their desire to be literal here because the Greek and English have two different aspects is understandable. While there is a distaste for "**Before Abraham came to be**, <u>I have been in existence</u>," it can be the preferred choice because it conveys the entire sense of what Jesus meant to convey, although it is ungrammatical in English. There is no theological baggage of trying to tie it to any other text, nor some avoidance of a grammar rule because it does not fit our preconceived ideas. One way to deal with the issue would be to adopt the dynamic equivalent rendering by K. L. McKay, "I have been in existence before Abraham was born."[38] However, the other alternative is to place the literal rendering in the main text of the Bible: Jesus said to them, "Truly, truly, I say to you, **before Abraham was** / *am*. Then, have an extensive footnote explaining the translation issues. This way the reader who desires to have the traditional reading is satisfied and the Bible is also making the translation issues available. Remember, though, our focus is to please God, not a translation committee, publisher, or reader.

---

[38] K. L. McKay, A New Syntax of the Verb in New Testament Greek, and the Gospel of John, 91.

CHRISTIAN PUBLISHING HOUSE
SCRIBES AND SCRIPTURE
FROM SPOKEN WORDS
TO SACRED TEXTS
INTRODUCTION-INTERMEDIATE
NEW TESTAMENT TEXTUAL STUDIES
EDWARD D. ANDREWS

FIRST TIMOTHY 2:12

WHAT DOES THE BIBLE REALLY SAY ABOUT WOMEN PASTORS/PREACHERS?

EDWARD D. ANDREWS

400,000+ SCRIBAL ERRORS IN THE GREEK NEW TESTAMENT MANUSCRIPTS

WHAT ASSURANCE DO WE HAVE THAT WE CAN TRUST THE BIBLE?

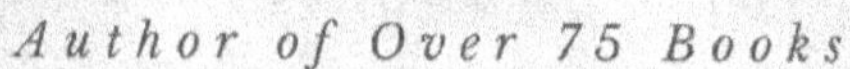

WHAT WILL HAPPEN IF YOU DIE?

EZEKIEL, DANIEL, & REVELATION

Bibliography

Arndt, William, Frederick W. Danker, and Walter Bauer. 2000. *A Greek-English Lexicon of the New Testament and Other Early Christian Literature. 3rd ed.* . Chicago: University of Chicago Press.

Arnold, Clinton E. 2002. *Zondervan Illustrated Bible Backgrounds Commentary Volume 2: John, Acts.* . Grand Rapids, MI: Zondervan.

Beekman, John, and John Callow. 1974. *Translating the Word of God.* Grand Rapids: Zondervan.

Brand, Chad, Charles Draper, and England Archie. 2003. *Holman Illustrated Bible Dictionary: Revised, Updated and Expanded.* Nashville, TN: Holman.

Bray, Gerald. 2010. *Translating the Bible: From William Tyndale to King James.* London: The Latimer Trust.

Carson, D. A. 1991. *The Gospel according to John, The Pillar New Testament Commentary.* Leicester, England; Grand Rapids, MI: Inter-Varsity Press; W.B. Eerdmans, 1991.

Edwards, Tyron. 1908. *A Dictionary of Thoughts.* Detroit: F. B. Dickerson Company.

Elwell, Walter A. 2001. *Evangelical Dictionary of Theology (Second Edition).* Grand Rapids: Baker Academic.

Elwell, Walter A, and Philip Wesley Comfort. 2001. *Tyndale Bible Dictionary.* Wheaton, Ill: Tyndale House Publishers.

Exell, Joseph S., and Thomas H. Leale. 1892. *Genesis, The Preacher's Complete Homiletic Commentary.* New York; London; Toronto: Funk & Wagnalls Company.

Gangel, Kenneth O. 2000. *Holman New Testament Commentary, vol. 4, John* . Nashville, TN: Broadman & Holman Publishers.

Keener, Craig S. 1993. *The IVP Bible Background Commentary: New Testament.* Downer Groves, IL: InterVarsity Press.

Metzger, Bruce. 2001. *The Bible in Translation: Ancient and English Versions.* Grand Rapids: Baker Academic.

Ryken, Leland. 2008. *Choosing a Bible: Understanding Bible Translation Differences.* Wheaton: Crossway Books.

—. 2009. *Understanding English Bible Translation: The Case for an Essentially Literal Approach.* Wheaton: Crossway Books.

Scorgie, Glen G, Mark L Strauss, and Stephen M Voth. 2003. *The Challenge of Bible Translation.* Grand Rapids: Zondervan.

Vine, W E. 1996. *Vine's Expository Dictionary of Old and New Testament Words.* Nashville: Thomas Nelson.

Wallace, Daniel B. 1999. *Greek Grammar Beyond the Basics – Exegetical Syntax of the New Testament.* Grand Rapids, MI: Zondervan Publishing House.

Wayne, Grudem, and Packer J. I. 2005. *Translating Truth: The Case for Essentially Literal Bible Translation.* Wheaton, IL: Good News Publishers/Crossway Books.

Westcott, Brooke Foss. 1908. *The Gospel according to St. John Introduction and Notes on the Authorized Version, Classic Commentaries on the Greek New Testament.* London: J. Murray,: J. Murray.

* 9 7 9 8 6 1 7 6 0 1 8 1 9 *